FALLOUT

Liam O'Meara CFC

Fallout

THE CHILDREN OF BELARUS
AND THE PEOPLE OF IRELAND
AFTER CHERNOBYL

the columba press

First published in 2003 by
the columba press
55A Spruce Avenue, Stillorgan Industrial Park,
Blackrock, Co Dublin

Cover by Bill Bolger
Origination by The Columba Press
Printed in Ireland by ColourBooks Ltd, Dublin

ISBN 1 85607 401 3

Contents

Introduction

Like so many more people in various homes and parishes throughout this land, we have been called to act by the smiles of children of Belarus. Quietly and gently they have entered our hearts. Quietly and gently, people in every part of the country have responded.

These children haven't come across the word 'victim'. They do not see themselves as victims of life, of place or of nuclear pollution. They rejoice. They are alive. Often, in their brokenness, they have more to offer us than we have to offer them. While we care for them, they bring life to our souls and joy to our hearts. They renegotiate important things within us. Important things for us to remember. Important things for our beautiful world.

This telling of some of their stories and our stories is simply that – an account of how we have been affected by the fallout from Chernobyl as visited upon us by the beauty of the children who have come into our hearts and homes.

It is meant as a tribute to our good people and to all the good people in the various Chernobyl groups throughout Ireland, as well as to all who help and support in so many ways. It is a word of thanks to all the directors and the workers in the orphanages who have welcomed us and accepted our intrusion into their lives. Above all, it is written as a tribute of thanks to the children, in the hope that we might continue to respond to little ones whose lives and souls are constantly in danger.

It is a remembering that we have a godbeat within us and that as such our only possibililty is to repsond in love. That the darkness within us might become as bright as day and that the light within us be set free.

CHAPTER ONE

There has to be something else

Fragments from the nuclear explosion fallout at Chernobyl station, which blew into the sky on 26 April 1986, landed on us. At first we heard only of rain clouds, of winds bringing devastation, of animals contaminated by radiation. We were told – don't go there; not if you are young, or pregnant, or ever want to be pregnant; not unless you want to come back with two heads, several cancers and the likelihood of more. Don't go there.

But we went anyway.

We were requested to take with us several golf balls so that on our return our friends could play Lahinch links in the dark, following the glow of the contaminated radiated Titleist into the Dell, through the Klondike and eventually back up the long eighteenth towards the clubhouse. Birdie. Birdie. Eagle. In the dark.

But in Belarus it is no joke.

We were told that whatever you do, don't eat the mushrooms and stay away from the berries. Don't drink any of the water and don't wash yourself anywhere outside of Minsk, the capital. We were told to bring enough of everything to last us whatever length we were going to be in this devastated land. And we were warned that whatever else we forgot, not to forget the all-important toilet paper.

We sat beside the magnificent cascades down the Archway in Ennistymon and watched the power of the Irish summer liquid sunshine force its rushed way past the Falls Hotel to relieve itself into the sea further down. What a magnificent living postcard of beauty! And a time to consider how simple it would be to destroy this our world. A time to imagine the unique Burren destroyed. Could it happen here as it had happened in the world we had been warned to avoid?

But we could not avoid this stained world. The fragments of fallout resounded somewhere in the chambers of our hearts. The

quiet appeal of an unknown child speaking a foreign language
or none, in a faraway contaminated country, seeped under the
doorways of our hearts and was enough to pluck us away from
our own comforts.

We had to go. And so we did. First we became aware of important things about ourselves – a certain steely determination
to be part of a solution to a problem we did not understand; a
fine curiosity to find out some truths; an uncertain minor ambi-
tion to try to follow a trek where no one had gone before; and an
inner belief of some strength in our own faith and in our work
and in the responsibility we all have for this gentle, beautiful
planet.

As we went we discovered the importance of that sense of
ourselves. We learned to say, somewhere in the quietness of our
own personal determination and tiredness, that I am what I believe. That what I believe is what I am. That who I am comes to
life and finds vigour in what I do – what I do for myself, for others
and, as we began this new work, what I do for the handicapped
special-needs people. We found that living out our belief
brought us to work with such special children. Children who
have taught us what love is. Children who have fingertip-
touched in our hearts every fibre of sensitivity and nurtured
within us new life where fear of reaching out had once begun to
sprout roots. Places that we didn't know existed now began to
affect us. Places within us are now affected by the smiles and
tugs of special children, children with the ability and the chance
to do nothing but smile. From under the blanket of gentle darkness in our hearts, the shoots of life have begun to sprout.
Together, the script of our lives within us comes to life, and is
written.

Of whom am I talking? We had a few children come and stay
a while with us, visit school for a little and then disappear into
the fog somewhere, wherever Chernobyl or Belarus or the great
Russia exists. Somewhere out there beyond the limited edges of
the Moher cliffs of our minds. A strange language and a strange
connection through the mists of nuclear disaster which we really
didn't understand and which seemed somehow too big and far
away. And yet these children and their needs seeped into our
lives, under the doorways of our schools and homes where they

first arrived to make our homes their homes. Our hearts became expanded nests where they could snuggle for a while before the airport-departure agony, which saw them flying off again, back to their contaminated world. They flew away from us to a world almost inaccessible, as Russian telephone operators had little patience for foreigners; inaccessible as the letters sent rarely seemed to arrive. Even when they did, the returned answers in 'joined writin' Russian was a problem which even I as a teacher could not often decipher.

Of course, a first trip to Belarus had to be made, a trip not without incident and danger. Having finally worked out that the wretched place lay somewhere on the other side of Poland we felt we had some reasonable idea of where at least we would end up. A three and a half hour flight from Shannon Airport seemed very short to us as, in our minds, this land existed way beyond Iron Curtains and Russian Bears and, of course, would be shrouded in a glorious haze of vodka. A bit fell off the plane. Tupalov 154. Yes, as we took off in the early Shannon morning, stewardess and pilot in their turn came back to look out the rear side window near where we were sitting to see what was not outside that should have been outside. We felt it was taking an impossibly long time to gain altitude – looking forward as we were to getting a glimpse of the sun above the clouds, if it still existed – and began to realise that something was amiss. So we continued with our Hail Marys but were eventually forced to turn about and land. None of the flight staff felt it might be nec-essary or even polite to inform us travellers that there was a change of plan or a problem. No one pointed out that we were going to re-land, certainly not in English. So we gazed out the windows photographing the ambulances and fire-engines chasing us down the runway, blissfully unaware of the bit of the engine that had lately dove, as the Americans say, without parachute or bungee rope into the boggy bed that is Rineanna.

Twelve hours later we made a second attempt and this time, whether because it was dark and no-one could see bits falling off or whether the plane actually hung together – or because after twelve duty-free hours we simply didn't give a tosser – we headed out once more eastwards for Belarus. A minus eighteen freezing night bearhugged us on arrival and didn't let go. It was

the warmest greeting we got as the Russian Bord Fáilte has yet
to be established. So, the stony cold of the granite international
airport matched beautifully the cold faces of the Passportnik
control officers, the baggagenik luggage people and the mili-
tary-headed militsia with their Khalashnikovs. A nice, pleasant
introduction to our first encounter with Russian officialdom!

It took a mere two hours for the seven of us to be passed
through the arrivals procedure. First, passport control. Then,
customs declaration form to be filled out in either German or
Russian as no English language versions were available. Then
wait for the baggage to come through and carry it, haul it, push
it through ahead of you, as the two luggage trolleys were already grabbed by someone else. And then the worst was over.
Or so we thought! It was now about four o'clock in the morning
and we had just come through into the crisp morning air. Into
our war-relic, minibus-type vehicle, bags and coats safely
loaded into the back and away we went, three of us to Luninets
and the others off towards Gomel. Trees and trees and trees,
laden beautifully with fatfolds of snow, shepherded us through
the night. The moon a silken, ivory sheen all about. Gorgeous.
Like a living Christmas card. But it was only October. The blasted
heater didn't work! On and on we went through the cold. No
idea how to say to whoever was driving – probably Sasha – that
we were perished and that our coats were in the back and that
would he ever for feck's sake turn on the blasted heater. Brian
stretched out and in time honoured fashion removed his boots.
Thanks, Brian. Every contribution acknowledged. Somewhere
in a bag there was a little bottle of Jameson, a possible present
for whoever we would meet – if we lived to meet anyone.
Maybe he wouldn't notice one slug gone out of it? Or two?
Maybe I should pass it round? But, there they were, feeding
away from a selection of brandy and other bottles. We just might
survive!

Two old ladies, well-layered with clothes and hunched over
their twig-brushes, were sweeping the leaves from the snow and
hacking ice from the steps of a building as we arrived early-
morning into Luninets. Busy morning! People hurrying on foot
to work – or not to work. Who knows? Meet interpreter. Brian
heads off. Patrick and I, hawing whiskey, stare open-mouthed

out the back of the van as Brian was the only one who knew
Russian and there he was heading off into some huge maze of a
dom as we sat unable, unknowing and not at all sure what to do.
(I should add that Brian's knowledge of Russian amounted to
tea, toilet and an attempt at hello – but it was still a considerable
lot more than we two had between us.)

I was lead to the house where I would be staying, home of
Gena and Irina. Lovely people. No English, no French. They had
a little German but I had none. A room with a bed. This must be
mine. Frozen and brittle, I eased myself in under the blanket,
having removed my boots from the ice sticks that were once my
legs. Still chattering with the cold, afraid that I will break in two
with the shivering. A knock immediately calls me to breakfast.
There they are, two little dotes! Two soft, runny eggs sitting on a
white plate, looking up at me, the yellow yellow, the white see-
through, like frogspawn that we used fish from the pond and
bring to school in jamjars long ago when we were small and
Angela's ashes were still hot (damp) coals! My breakfast – in a
strange house, with people who can't speak any language I
know, after an all night journey in a freezing van, with Brian's
socks and no sleep, several sips from a Jemmy bottle – and here
they are! This'll test you. Gena and Irina sit opposite me, watching. Smiles, concern and ready to greet me in traditional Russian
fashion with breakfast and Vodka! Jesus, Mary and Joseph!
Vodka is bad enough but for breakfast and with two raw, smiley
eggs to follow. It'll take some doing!

'It's lovely, thanks very much. I love fried eggs. Runny.
Vodka? No thanks! Oh! All right then seeing as you have it
poured. Are you having one yourself? Three? Three vodkas? For
breakfast? With two raw eggs! Sure you wouldn't have it in the
Falls!' (Damned sure you wouldn't). Such lovely people. Giving
me all they had, as I later understood. They were delighted to
welcome a foreigner into their home. We chatted a little with the
use of a dictionary. Letter? Yes. Write? Yes, sure I will. And so
on.

I was sick until Wednesday.

It was the first of many trips. To be soaked up and later di-
gested. Landmarks of time and feeling bright on the horizon of
our inner eye. Answers feeling right. A sense of the place being

part of us. Feeling in a strangely-recognised way at home. As a place we had once been and would be again. A place lived in perhaps in a former life, a *deja-vu* home with recognisable tastes and smells. A feel of homecoming – but all that later in the private recesses of our minds. Now, a simple sense of the tug of the place.

Each trip was also full of the unknown and laden with new experiences and wonderful people. Mostly these trips became centred on the children, especially the children of two orphanages for physically and mentally handicapped children – the children of Cherven and, later, of Goradishche orphanage. It was in these *internats* that we came face to face with what we are really all about. Who we are. What we believe. What we must do. And it was here we came to know these forgotten children as a challenge and as a chance. A challenge to see beyond the immediate situation. A chance to see within ourselves what we have been made for and to know the love-granite from which we have been hewn. Only here to recognise the corner stone of ourselves. The visit was a time to cry, to feel pain and to get to know the hurt of loving children in a way we never expected. Perhaps, in a way we never wanted.

Yet, these children came into our lives and into our hearts. There, they have nestled, rooted and disturbed us into action to try to make life a little better for them in their current situation. Moments with the children are special. It is like listening to Sonia O'Brien on the fiddle. Living the music. Big-smiling the smile. It was as if the tuning of our hearts suddenly hummed into life within us and, in our hearts, the butterfly-wing of vibration continued to fan into life the Eden-experience of love. It was a going back and a going forward. This in a way that we would not run from but would rather recognise and come willingly forward. Yes, I felt I do not know what to do; I know nothing about handicapped children; I am inadequate to the needs. But enter in we did. Tenderly, humbly, gently in the open embrace of the smiles of these very special children in these orphanages for the unwanted.

There are some very good memories of that early trip. I remember heading east towards the contaminated zone. As we passed a sign for Hoiniki, I remember Patrick saying that his two

children were from there. It was down a long road, strange looking in Russian script. We tried to work out the Russian letters
but were gone past before we got to the end of the name on the
signpost. We passed the crossroads and kept going. Patrick was
referring to the two children he had hosted in Ireland previously.
Now, somewhere out there in the dim, distant, radiated environment two children lived a life which had for one little while
shared in the Camelot that is the foothills of Mulloughmore.

Later, Patrick told us of his ferocious battle with the local
tradition of toasting with vodka. First toast to our meeting. Then
to friendship. Then to love. Then to women. Then to whatever
you want. Having never taken a drink in his life, it was surpris-
ing to meet up with him at the end of the day and hear him recall
(barely) how he had managed to limit his intake of vodka that
day to just fourteen 'chootchoots'. 'Avoiding vodka here,' he
said, 'is like avoiding rain in Ireland.' True, especially when the
day includes a visit to the famous Russian custom of sauna,
where instead of water, beer is thrown on the rocks and they use
bunches of birch twigs on naked butts and bodies to stimulate
the circulation. They take an occasional pause in the proceed-
ings to top up with vodka and the odd bit of food. Vodka good!
Good for 'flu, good for cold and now, in a new role, good for
radiation!

This was our first experience of what the country and the
people were like. It was the first defrosting in the freezing cold
of something vital within us. In going to this contaminated land,
we recognized and felt within ourselves a call, a nudge, a tug not
to abandon and forget. In our visits, we just simply heard a tune
we knew, echoing to the toetap of our hearts.

This was just the first of many trips. Trips which would take
us into shadowy places and whispery lives in a world new to us.
Spending a week in a country gave a flavour of the place but to
get to know a people takes much longer. As our group, the
Burren Chernobyl Project, developed its plans to help out in
Belarus, it was necessary to get a fuller sense of how this country
works. We needed to know if the relics of the recently-fallen
communist system had in fact been replaced or just renamed. It
was time to go and abide there a while.

CHAPTER TWO

Getting to know the place

So, I decided to take a year off school and go there. Simply head off and see what would transpire. To wander off like John the Baptist into this desert place. Robed, seeking honey, prepared for a taste of wild locust or whatever local dish the trip might throw up for me. (It threw up lots of porridge-type stuff and the occasional chicken's toes at the bottom of a bowl of soup!) My year off school would, therefore, be a time to explore this world, to experience it first hand, to boldly go where I had never thought of going before.

In my enthusiasm, I didn't even figure that not speaking Russian might be a problem. So, on arrival, I stood outside Minsk International Airport waiting to be met by people I had come across on the previous trip. The local text-lite sign announced that it was minus nineteen and it didn't feel like a thaw was about to set in. Not having the language proved to be interesting. First, people spoke to me. Then when I looked on making no reply, they shouted at me. Then they gave up, realising how stupid I must be!

This was the day after Mission Sunday. A thought for the day spoke of 'leaving behind the familiar smells, the nets in place … and all the companions of my former life … when it was too late to go back I found myself drowning between two lives, the one I was trying to leave, the one I was trying to follow.' That pretty well described my situation exactly. And if the good Lord did not stretch out his hand, like Peter, I would be pushed to the limits of my spiritual doggy-paddle.

On this trip there was time to visit several orphanages and villages. Firstly, I went to Yastrebel. A chance to check out a relatively good orphanage. Here to make contact with Lyonya and little Sasha who would become regular visitors to Ennistymon. Later I moved to visit Kobrin, to experience a well-run children's village in a scheme sponsored by the Germans. Here, a group of

16

children live as a family in a very well-built house and they have the care and protection of House Mothers to look after them all. These are for healthy, 'normal' children. It was all interesting, finding storage space in the back of my mind, waiting proper assessment of whether these places would be the ones that we would commit to. But, there was more to see.

Eventually I found myself in Gomel, the second city of Belarus in the south-east corner, nearest large population centre to where the Chernobyl Reactor had exploded across the border in the Ukraine. Meeting up with some natives, I got the chance to travel with them and visit some of the seriously-contaminated local areas. One day we went to Vetka, a small town not far from Gomel. Basically, an evacuated town where fine houses lie empty, abandoned, idle; windows reflecting wide-eyed surprise at the sudden departure. Only old women and mad ones live here now, they say. Old women who refused to move to live in other areas, mad ones whom no-one wants and perhaps who know no different. This is a long, abandoned, lonely, lonely place. Yet, apples grow in profusion on contaminated trees. They tell me that this Vetka was a golden, delicious place, the new Moscow. When believers were banished from Moscow, they came to live in Vetka. This was the place to come to, the place of refuge for believers, the road back to God, the way to heaven. And then Chernobyl sprays its contamination over every bird and beast, over every living thing. The cradle of the Lord, the 'way' is struck, covered, polluted with the deadly fallout from Chernobyl. This is, then, not just the destruction of a town. It is a blow at the nexus. It is the fission of spirituality in Belarus. The holy way is stricken from above. In the centre, the hall is full of icons in a terror-town stricken from above as other towns about lie in relative safety.

In some building somewhere in my memory, a little girl sits at an old loom and they plan to sell her products in time. Backwards they move into the future. Walking through these streets was like walking through Ireland of eighteen forty-five, six and seven condensed. Hearing the schoolsilent voices of the disappeared. Hearing the backwash of spiritual adrenalin as hope is consumed, changed into something like hope but not hope, something else. It was like living in a mirror where everything seems normal and appears to work, but is merely a dying shadow of what it should be, of reality. The spirit of this place is hurting. Maybe, it is even beyond sensation. Contaminated by an enemy that cannot be seen, touched, felt, tasted or smelt; one that cannot be stopped. And yet here, I feel the throb of need and humanity bruised. Not yet time to turn off the ventilator though here all is somehow lifeless.

Some days later, I went to visit a family in Mozir, another town in the armpit of Chernobyl. The son from this family had spent a holiday in Ireland and the Irish family had asked me to call in to see him if I was anywhere near. I was just making contact to see how things were. Someone had phoned from the city of Gomel to tell this family I would be arriving. I was put on a bus in Gomel and someone on the bus was asked to make sure that I got off at the right place. As the bus arrived exhausted into Mozir, a woman with a bunch of flowers and her son were waiting for me. She is especially pleased to see me and is in tears as she talks on about what I assume is her son's trip to Ireland and her tears are a measure of her thanks to those who had helped. The government is very poor here and acted very poorly in the early, critical days of Chernobyl fallout. When the fallout was falling out, Luda was seven months pregnant, yet for eight days she worked in the contamination, unaware of the terrible death that was landing all about her – unaware of what it was doing to herself, unaware of what it was doing to her son. Only when the officials and government officers began to depart did the people *en masse* begin to realise that something was seriously wrong. Then finally a public announcement: get on a bus and leave with nothing but your passport. This was the stark announcement. Leave with nothing. Just get out. To this day, the insensitivity, the ignorance and the blatant disregard brings ready tears to the eyes of the people who knew no better. People who accepted the word of the powers that be. They were used to being told what to do. The state would look after them. This is also a part of the tragedy of Chernobyl. The people believed in the system. They believed the system would provide for them and protect them. But, the system, the state, took off and left the people behind. As Tatiana later said: 'It was all a lie.' And now, with everything shattered around, what is there to believe?

It was while I was visiting this house in Mozir, that a small event occurred which would have a huge consequence later on. A phone call. Just as I had arrived to the house for the first time, the phone rang. It was for me. I remember thinking: 'How can it be for me. I don't know where I am. How can anybody else know where I am?' On the end of the line was Maria Mitskevich, a lady from Minsk. She runs a fund which tries to get children out, tries to get them away from the contaminated zone which is now their home. Maria was looking for Liam. As it turned out, I was the wrong Liam. However, we arranged to meet back in Minsk whenever I got there. It was from that simple wrong phonecall that I later met Maria and she lead me and our group to Cherven Orphanage for the mentally and physically handicapped. Later she would lead us to Goradishche. At this stage we knew nothing about the future. It was only later we reflected that had I been called Harry or Tom or anything else but Liam, life would have taken a different direction. The Liam that Maria sought may have been Liam Grant who has for many years been doing wonderful work in Belarus. The Liam that Maria found was me and that has made all the difference.

The Burren Chernobyl Project had been working bringing some children to Clare for rest and rehabilitation. Some had come for six months to stay and learn English, attending school and undergoing homeopathic treatment for radiation and its effects. Other children had come from good orphanages for holidays and whatever medical care they required. Yet, there was something more we needed to do. Something we wanted to do – to reach the ones that no-one was helping, to find the ones most in need, to try to make a difference to the lives of the unwanted.

So, my time off school in Ireland had been spent in Belarus seeking out something. Something of which we weren't sure. It was a search in the hope of finding something vital, some place where we were really needed. Hopefully, it was a search in the right place. Wandering around Belarus was all very interesting. It was time to make contact. Time to make a connection. It was time to be led where we were needed. As the time passed away and the thoughts of returning home came into my mind, I headed for Minsk to spend a few days there. It was time to get back in touch with hot water and supermarkets, time for a good wash and a walk about town. It was a time to meet Maria, the lady on the other end of the phoneline, the lady who wanted to contact Liam.

It was my last day before returning home. It was Maria who said that perhaps I might visit Cherven Orphanage and perhaps do something to help. Why not? Let's go. It was thus through Maria's contact and invitation that I was brought from Minsk to Cherven on 21 May 1997 to see what we might do. It was the day before I left for Ireland.

It was a trip like any other trip. A car from Minsk. Only an hour out the road. I hardly recognized it then, but something stirred. Something came to life. It was like John O'Donoghue's *anamchara* gently echoing an eternal whispering once more. It was a beginning. A journey begun. Leading somewhere. I wasn't sure where but I went.

As Mark says: come and see. So I went and this is what I saw.

CHAPTER THREE

I know who you are

I don't know if it was a boy or a girl. I thought it was a girl but I was afraid to touch her. She was wrapped in a strait-jacket type thing, like having a shirt on back to front, and she couldn't move her hands to scratch the sore on her head – a big open sore with some sort of green powder on it. She was just one of the children in the orphanage.

The strongest memory is the smell of the place. Toilets and beds and kitchen, it was hard to know which was worst. I'd been to some bad places before but this time I'd just gone to see. There were to be no emotions and no upset; just go and see and make a report. It's hard to be a rock in some places but that is what I decided to be.

As I passed through the rooms of the orphanage, I tried to ensure that I touched each and every child. I didn't know anything about handicapped children but it seemed wrong to touch some, to smile and then not to spend time with others. There are two hundred and fifty of them altogether. About fifty-five children lie in bed all the time. The people who were showing me round said I was the first visitor to actually touch the children. And pick them up. They lay in the beds where they have lain for all their lives and they smiled when I touched them under the chin.

They arched up to feel the touch and they laughed with bright smiles at the feel. Their eyes didn't find me, they just lay there and stared into space, unseeing. But they felt and responded and I thought isn't it awfully easy to change someone's life, just to give a child bound to a bed a rub under the chin. And I think I was frightened.

There is no way to bring back just how awful these places are. You just have to go there and pretend to be a stone with no feelings and bury it under your subconscious somewhere and make-believe to move along without any feeling. Knowing that you will have to deal with it later, somewhere else. It must be awful to work there in these conditions. I don't think I could cope with this every day. In these conditions.

They are in an old building used for horses during the Great Patriotic War but good enough now for discarded and handicapped children. The kind of place where you take a deep breath outside the door and hope you will get through the smell and that your breath will last until you get back out again. I pass along between the rows of beds and wonder where is the madness of this world – in the heads of these children who smile and light up when I touch them, or is the madness in a world which still allows this kind of thing to exist? And it is only over the wall, only over the wall from Europe with its mountains and lakes of excess.

The owners of the mountains and the guardians of those lakes will do nothing to impact on these children. They will simply continue as they have done. It seems that as we get richer we have forgotten the words of Montaigne who said: 'No matter how high you build your throne, you still sit on your arse.' And so I think of Rita Kenny, and all the Rita Kennys of this world, who gave me twenty pounds out of her pension for these children and I think of the thousands that have gone astray into places that perhaps do not need it, places to entertain and amuse us in our wealth and richness. And I think that as the world gets richer, I will have to rely on the pounds of my friends such as the bingo players to feed, to clothe, to wash these foreign, forgotten children because ours is a world where only the little people really care and understand. The people who have been to the margins. People who want to make a difference.

And the children still smile back up at me and all I can do is rub their chins and pretend that I can cope with this. And I cannot. I cannot cope with this. I cannot cope with children who've lived all their lives in bed. I cannot cope with enamel buckets of slop that pass for food, rattling along behind me down the corridors. I cannot cope with the smell. Yet, I cannot walk from here and keep this heart-hardness within me. I cannot walk away and leave these living smiles behind me. I cannot leave these hidden children for God's sake, buried here in this dreadful place.

It was Alexander who asked, please if you can, do something. You picked up the children, he said. The children came to you, wanted to be picked up. This is a good sign. Please, if you can, do something. But Jesus Christ, how do I ... how can I know what to do? The place needs to be knocked to the ground, buried deep and forgotten. Oh how I want to bring these children home to Clare, to people who will pick them up, wash their sores and just hold them and see their smiles.

Why do mentally handicapped children smile? Why do children with only physical handicap smile for me when they have been dumped into a mental asylum all their lives? And yet they smile! Why do they smile? What is there to smile about? No education, no hugs, no clean clothes, no touch. And when I touch them, they come alive. Or is it I who have begun to hear again and to see again in the midst of all this handicap?

Oh for the Pats and the Anns and the Phils and the Marys and the Nualas and the Paddys of Clare. Oh for the mothers and fathers of Clare who would come in here with buckets and mops and paint and brushes and hugs and love and care and tears. But I am here now alone and what to do?

Fifty-four of them have never been anywhere but in bed. Some of them are small and thin, bundles almost lost in blankets. Shaved head and listless eyes stare as I pass. Others have spent all their lives in one room. This room is their world. A song says: 'If I died and woke up in a world like ours, I'd think I was in heaven.' If these children died and woke up in a world like theirs! A dull dreary room, full of packed-together beds with a ceiling for a sky, no breeze on their cheeks, no wind through their hair, no sunshine on their shoulders. No love story here.

Yet the smile of Natasha was full of excitement and lit up the room. I hope I will never forget it. She has spent all her life in this bed, first bed inside the door of group five, lined up beside Tamara, side by side in a room of twenty-eight beds. This is her world and this is the red book of her life. 'At the age of birth you were rejected by your mother ... no account of your father. It appears he was more interested in Vodka ... At the age of one month you were placed here in a bed ... This is your life.' It is unfair of course to blame but where are the parents? Where are the parents? The mothers? The fathers? Where are the Mrs. Browns? Christy, was it like this for you?

Vova is five and his face, squashed in on one side, has an ear badly out of place on his jaw due to some birth difficulty. So he is dumped here. He follows me and sucks his thumb, a grubby half-face, dirty and dishevelled. And I think that were all our defects on the outside, obvious, we'd all be in asylums.

In these situations one has to reflect. To get over the revulsion and to reflect. One has to turn off the switches which say I will be sick at the smell, I will be repulsed by the disfigurement, I will be offended at the enormity of it all. And only then can one pass through and see the people themselves, see the children as children. And feel the gospel opening of our ears and eyes. It is impossible to pass through and not feel that important things are being asked and questioned. For me, these were stirring moments. Meeting with these children in their isolated situation touched something deeply emotional within me. There was of course the stench of human waste and the smells of people who are always indoors. But for me there was also the shock understanding that these children are people. I tried to remember what I had been teaching back home in school in Ennistymon about everyone's rights. Rights we needn't remember as we take them for granted. Rights which don't exist for these children. They are basic rights. But what are they? The right to life. The right to dignity. They have the right to reasonable comfort. The right to reach their potential whatever it may be. And I felt ashamed that I couldn't even remember the obvious, the taken-for-granted rights which we all have.

The sheer size of the numbers, the sub-level at which they live and the attitude which seemed not to value them, were almost too much to take in at once. I spent weeks later not sleeping but just seeing them and knowing that somehow I would be linked with these children into the future and that it was a challenge and an opportunity not to be walked away from.

Why? Simply because these were children in need and the echoes of their calling out to the spirit of the universe had by some roundabout way brought me from my comfort zone into this place. And perhaps in this place I recognised something of myself and found a comfort zone again. Here there is no hiding, there is absolutely no shame. When everything you need depends on someone else, there can be no shame.

There is no shame in being disfigured, in being unable to walk or talk, in being without any of what our world thinks is important. In many senses it is a better place, a healthier place to live. In our modern world, someone is always telling us what to drink, what to eat, what shape to be, what to wear and how to smell. Greedy big businesses spend millions of pounds each year trying to make me buy something that will swell their bank account and increase their sales. But that doesn't matter here. What matters now is only my response, what am I going to do about it? The children of Belarus ask with their eyes only that I come into the room, that I spend time with them, that I accept them as they are, as indeed they accepted me and all the others who came. No expectations, no demands, no shame. No call on big important people to do something. Just a call to us. And so on my return home I had to say that the situation demanded a lot of help. I felt unable to cope with it, I simply didn't know what to do. Or where to begin. I began by asking for help, asking people to read the story of what I saw, the story of the children. I had to ask for help and wait like the children in the hope that someone was listening and would respond.

So I wrote:

'Now if you read this and have read this far, know this, I need your help. I simply need your help with this. I am acting as interpreter for fifty four children who cannot talk to you and one hundred and ninety-six others, who simply know how to smile. And what they say is: 'Please , if you can, help. And if you have no time or are too busy, don't worry, we will make no further demands on you. We will lie here as we have lain all our lives and wait. And when next a visitor comes through we will again smile out our plea and keep on smiling because we are handicapped, we have mental problems and we know no better, just to smile and wait and smile for you.'

I thought I was asking people of Ennistymon and roundabout to help. Only then did I see it as a call from the Spirit of the Universe, a call from the eternal echoes asking us to respond and not to walk away. And so this is not just my call for help to other people. It is my experience of what I am asked to do by the Keeper of the Garden, a Keeper long held to be all powerful but within this world also dependent on those who can give a hand in special places and in difficult times. It is the why of life. And He/She says to me:

> 'Know this. I need your help, I simply need your help with this. Please if you can, help. And if you have no time or are too busy, don't worry, I will make no further demands on you. I simply need your help.'

It was Mike who said the song would be a good one for us, a good theme song. It is so suitable, the words we could take to heart, words to remember and to hold on to, words that give life and bring joy:

> Little darling , here comes the sun,
> Little darling , the smile's returning to their faces
> Little darling , it seems like years since it's been there
> Little darling.

But now as I sit and try to write this, it is only now that I cry the tears that should have flowed long ago, tears of shattering shock for what I've forgotten – important things about how we should live and how I have stopped listening to my own spirit – tears of unknowing where to go from here and tears which clean from my sight the nonsense and trivia which so surrounds us in this our present heaven. And now, I see before me the children who have never left their beds, who have never been outdoors, who have never sat on their mother's knee.

And still they smile ... why? Wouldn't it make you wonder!

CHAPTER FOUR

He reached out his hand and touched

Group 6 was and still is one of the most difficult groups in the orphanage. Twenty-five children live here. They are difficult. Difficult behaviour and difficult because there is no plan to cope with them, no facilities to make their life better. There is no way that any of these children will get a chance to improve or to find some purposeful place in life. The children range from the very disturbed to some who are not quite so bad. It was here in this group that I first came across Alosha. It was in a crowded room with nothing happening for these children. I remember the bare green walls. I remember the children huddled like wet hens against the radiators trying to stay warm. I remember the little autistic boy Alosha with his legs crossed over one another and his forehead on the floor. He was wet and in his mind he was gone some place else. Why wouldn't he? At this stage I knew nothing about handicap or autism. I only knew that this guy, this strange faraway child, had to be looked after. Why he should be the one to leave an impression is hard to say. He looked like an old man, like Elmur Fudd in the Bugs Bunny cartoon or someone strangely familiar.

We decided to bring some children from group six to Ireland in the first of the trips. This group included the 'terrible twins', Artur and Radion, who both had the lovely habit of regurgitation of their food and who banged their heads off the walls or the doors when they didn't get food when they wanted it. They would literally take the bit out of your mouth or the mouth of another child.

Luckily for Alosha he endeared himself to us because of his being so difficult. In time Pat and Neilus would take him and begin a relationship that would make a difference to all our lives. Alosha is a success story. He is now back with his family, where all the children should be. This is part of his story with us.

If you want to make me clean, you can do it.
Big ears, Skinny. Cleft palate. Sitting cross legged. Forehead on
the floor. Green room. Group six. Cherven. Wet. By the radiator.
On a red mat. Pain in his watery eyes. Eyes which do not make
contact. Head-banging. Whinge. Legs folded neatly. Alosha.
   *Normal ears. Chubby. Sitting cross legged. Upright. Sitting room.
   Pat's house. Dry and clean. Blond, blue-eyed, smiler. Eye-contact.
   Cleft palate operation complete. Alosha.*

It is unbelievable, the transformation. Literally we found Alosha
in group six and something about him in his wretched state
more than the others registered and caused him to stay in my
memory. So awful! Wet and in tatters. Banging his head off the
wall or clattering himself with his open hand. No response to
calling his name. Just sitting there, legs-folded in his own world.
   He was one of the first we brought to Ireland, in the early
days when we didn't know what to do or what needed to be
done. They arrived in October 1997, a group of eight of the most
difficult to manage. Difficult because they were mobile and
needed attention all the time. Difficult because it was our first
experience of working with them.
   Alosha arrived into the monastery kitchen. Kathleen had
food ready. Alosha was ready for food. Grabbed and stuffed
into his mouth. Slices of bread and whatever else was in reach.
The sheer starvation of the child frightened us. He just grabbed
and gorged. We weren't ready for this. We weren't ready for the
implications which suggested that these children lived in
hunger, constantly. We weren't ready for the clear sign that in
order to get food in Alosha's world you grabbed first and asked
no questions. We managed to sit him at the table and give him a
portion for himself. Later we would learn that it was better to
feed him alone where he could leave aside the fear of not getting
any food and concentrate on eating. Due to his cleft-palate problem the food drooled down his nose. He cleaned the plate with
his fingers. Then he began to clean up every crumb off the table.
Then after wetting his fingers he began to comb his clothes for
any possible remaining crumb. A quick flick of his hand picked
a crumb from the face of a boy opposite. Then he clattered his
head, right side. Severely. And cried. We were afraid to give him

too much as we realised the situation. Again it was frightening. Rabid. Unexpected. And strange in that Alosha didn't speak and we had to try to understand his actions without language. What did he want? More? Drink? And so began our journey with him.

They were two difficult weeks. Observing, trying to understand. Feed Alosha on his own. Don't let Alosha see the others eating. No stress. Ok. Ok. Ok, pet. Don't worry. There's plenty. Just hold on a sec. Here, here, here you are. Easy, easy, easy. Autism! This was our first encounter with it. A strange condition in that the person with it can live within himself. Communication is difficult. For Alosha there were no words, no speech. We desperately wanted to understand. But, God, the amount of patience it required. We learned not to get frightened, bothered or upset when he was in one of his tantrums. And sometimes they were severe. We tried and tried to understand. To watch for the signs, to recognise his patterns of behaviour. To come to some sort of understanding of what was happening in his poor, clattered little head.

Pat and Neilus did enormous work with him. They decided to bring him back for six months, to try and build him up for a cleft-palate operation if that was possible. Build-up, operation, recovery. Six months. It would perhaps be the one great chance of his life. Millions of light years away from sitting by the radiator in group six with his forehead on the pee-wet floor. Away.

Big dirty nappy. He rocked in it and so it went up his back, down his legs. On the sheets, pillow, sometimes on the wall. The little angel. If only we could toilet-train him. Maybe if we learn to recognise his toilet routine we can get him on a potty in time. It was a tough six months especially at the start. Pat and Neilus did fabulous work with him. At first he could walk very little. He waited to be picked up and carried. By the end of his training session of six months on Lahinch beach, he had built up and become strong and could walk all the way down to the river and back again, in his little old man rocky shuffle, sometimes balanced, sometimes with a mad dash, right leg leading.

At first we had little communication. Bit by bit we recognised his ways. He had terrible tantrums. Banged his head and clattered himself and shut himself off in his room on his own. Usually we'd find him with the taps running and every drop of hot water in the house gone down the sink. He loved to sit in the toilet, flush it and sit cross-legged listening to the cistern fill up or even *feel* the water filling up. Then he'd flush again and sit listening and seemingly responding to the sounds of the toilet. Pat noticed how he began a tantrum by beginning to slap his hand. We noticed that there were a few reasons for tantrums. Maybe he was hungry, maybe he needed a drink, maybe he needed a walk, maybe he was dirty. By watching for the onset of the tantrum we began to be able to predict what he wanted. Sometimes we got it right. Sometimes we failed miserably and frustratingly and could let him just work through his tantrum which sometimes went on a long time.

We began working on getting the toilet situation improved. Up to this a dirty nappy meant a complete change of clothes for him and a full shower. We all remember the day Br Willie picked Alosha up out of the bed to bring him out and then all we heard was 'Shit! Shit! Shit!' as Willie came in contact with the reality of dirty nappies leaking down his good trousers for per-haps the first time in his life. Size 6 Pampers were a great inven-tion.

Little by little we got Alosha to a potty before the job was done. In time we got him onto a toilet to do his business. I re-member one day he was on the toilet but turned round to play with the flush handle and did his business on the floor. When I went in to re-dress him I calmly said, 'Ah, Alosha, what are you at? That should be in there, not on the floor. That would be much better. Then you could flush away all you want, Ok?' And he stood there and big watery tears flowed down his cheeks and fell in big wet splashes, spattering my heart on the floor.

Slowly he began to recognise us and to respond with great glee and excitement when Pat returned from school or when Neilus arrived to take him for his walk. Day after day, regard-less of the weather they headed out to Lahinch to walk the prom and get the air. Their long experience in running the North Clare Athletic Club really stood to them. As their former student, Maria McMahon, represented Ireland in the Atlanta Olympics they slowly and with loving patience walked up and down the prom by the sea in Lahinch. Five thousand kilometres west of them, the cheers had gone up for the world's top class athletes

showing their skills. On the blustery promenade, another re-
markable achievement was being born. Unapplauded. Un-
heralded. No medals. No national anthems. But, step by step,
Alosha raised his own banner. Only the people of Clare know
what that means. His rubbery feet took him further and further.
Eventually he could go all the way down the beach to the river
and back again. It was Alosha's marathon. It was his proclaim-
ing his right to be. Alosha had arrived.

Now that Alosha was getting stronger we felt it time to think
about his cleft-palate operation. This would first mean getting
permission from the authorities and/or from his parents so we
had to make contact with them, even though we had not met
them up to this. Then, luckily we managed to get a booking with
Mr Orr in Our Lady's Hospital for Sick Children in Crumlin.
Visiting the hospital with Alosha was interesting. We stopped
half-way to Dublin at Granny Ryan's to feed and change him.
Susie kept Alosha busy as we had a cup of tea. Waiting in a hospital queue with Alosha was very interesting. We walked the
corridor. He sat. He began to get upset. We gave him a banana.
Quiet again. Then it began again. More walking. Then a needle
for a blood test which he hated. Then waiting in the corridor
again. More upset. This time the bribe was a yogurt. Then a big
dirty nappy followed by a full-blown head-banging, head-clat-
tering tantrum. The poor thing! A doctor asked us to keep him
quiet as we were disturbing him! What could we do? It was a
wait of several hours. Alosha did his best. For a long time he was
very quiet but, eventually, he could be contained no longer.
Finally we got to see the Doctor. He gave a look into Alosha's
mouth, said 'Don't worry, I can fix that.' and so the beginning
was made. By this stage Alosha was happily playing with his
friend the water tap in the corner of the room. All the way home
he was good. He loves the car. He wouldn't lie down and sleep.
He wanted to see everything.

The day for hospital admission arrived in November. He was
all kitted out and ready for action. Again the long road to
Dublin. We stayed in the nearby Christian Brothers in Drimnagh
Castle until Alosha was admitted that evening. After a bit of a
delay, a bed had become available in the hospital. Alosha was
uneasy in bed. The nurses felt they could look after him and so

Yulia, our interpreter, and I headed to get something to eat. Half an hour later when we got back to the monastery there was a message waiting calling us back to the hospital as Alosha was throwing a wobbly. Back we went and there he was happy as Larry up to his elbows in water at the sink with a fine pool all round him. To bed! Yogurts. Bananas. Biscuits. He took them all but didn't really settle. Yulia offered to spend the night with him. In the morning he would be prepared for surgery and go straight to theatre.

We went to bed somewhat nervously but quietly exuberant that all would go well next day for the operation. However, our hopes were dashed as it was only during the night that the staff realised just how difficult Alosha could be and they could not guarantee enough staff to provide proper post-operative care. So, eventually the surgeon arrived to break the bad news that they had decided to postpone the operation for the time being. Hopefully it would take place after Christmas, when both Alosha and the hospital might be better prepared.

We were so disappointed. But God is good. Who knows? Perhaps it is all for the best. We headed home. Five hour journey thinking and wondering and trying to find meaning in the delay. But we would hope for better things. Through the coming weeks we worked away with Alosha. More and more improvements took place. Days would pass without a tantrum. Toilet routine became more regular. Feeding time became more normal. Bit by bit he made improvements and got stronger. He put on weight and got more and more handsome. He spent all the Christmas holidays with Pat and Neilus and family and really settled in that time. He became more adjusted and normal – not without the occasional wobble naturally.

Again, the call came from the hospital and off we went. This time the agreement was that Alosha could stay at the Brothers in Drimnagh and come into hospital ready for the operation in the morning, in other words, fasting. Let it be said that Alosha likes his breakfast first thing in the morning and to go without might be interesting! All was well until we went down the corridor of St Joseph's ward and Alosha saw breakfast being given out. I moved to intervene but too slowly. He saw food. He wanted food. He couldn't have food. Fingers twitched. Tantrum starts. I begin to try to quieten him, then notice an added interest in the staff, they have just become aware of Alosha's presence, that he is special and needs attention. I pretended to quieten him but mentally said, 'Good on you, you tell them. You're here and you want attention.' Fairly quickly we got our room, the doctors arrived, a few questions, sedative and so began the journey to pre-operation room. Complete with ER-style cap and gown I watched him being knocked out and wheeled into theatre. I hoped we were doing right for him and prayed that all would go well. I put my full confidence in Dr Orr.

The wait began. About four hours later, Alosha finally was wheeled from recovery room and back the corridor to his ward. He now needed fulltime care. He hated the needles, the drip, the heart monitor, the entire situation even in his knocked-out sleep and he pulled and tugged at the tubes and wires attached to his hands. The poor thing! I did first watch. Nurses in and out regularly, checking, monitoring, watching. He settled somewhat. An odd turn. A pull at the wires. Half-awake. Still asleep. Later, Jean came on duty specially to keep an eye on Alosha. We sat and talked in the quiet of the hospital evening.

Yulia did the late watch and I relieved her again in the morning. How would he be in the morning? Would everything be Ok? Would it heal? Would he tear at it? Would it pain? How would he manage without food? No food for three days! Don't let him see anyone else eating!

It took just two days actually. Two days watching him, waiting with him, walking him up and down the corridor. Directing him away from anywhere where there was food, giving him time to get to know all the taps in the hospital corridor. And he was as good as gold. No tantrums. No clattering. Just calm acceptance. After a while, he was allowed yogurts. Gentle care and careful attention. We went for a little walk outside but he wasn't able for much and he just stopped and put out his arms to be lifted. I picked him up and carried him back in. He let his head snuggle into my shoulder. It spoke to me of trust and of acceptance. It was as though he knew.

On the next day, Sunday, we went home. That meant firstly walking from Crumlin Hospital along the road to the comfort of Br Rochford's hospitality with the Brothers in Drimnagh Castle.

Traffic was heavy and loud. Each passing car an Olympic cheer as Alosha lead on, his old man shuffle taking him every step of the way himself, focused, non-stop, all the way back to the house. I have never been as proud of anyone in my life as of Alosha on his determined long-walk from the hospital back to himself on that special Sunday. Everything was just so beautiful.

His first feed after the operation was funny. He couldn't get as much into his mouth as before. Surprise registered on his face. He didn't need to push the food back his throat any more as his mouth was now normal. And he became more and more normal also. No tantrums – except on rare occasions. No grabbing. And he settled more and more into family life. He loved Sinead rubbing his belly. Grunted and smiled at Triona when she asked 'Are you tired?' Headed up to share Colm's bed every morning after his breakfast. He became happier, laughed more and responded well.

The six months were up and so he had to go back. We knew he was better. Again not an easy decision but there are so many more children waiting a chance. Could we possibly contact his family? Maybe they could take him home for some time? It would be so awful if this blond, blue-eyed treasure just returned into the orphanage and continued as though nothing had happened! We had to contact his family. It was Ina, a beautiful lady working in the orphanage, who put it all together for us and for Alosha and for his family. And so it came to be. On Monday 27 March 2000, all the family arrived to meet us at the orphanage in Cherven. Mother, auntie, brother, cousin, granny and grandad, all arrived into the orphanage to meet us on that morning. It was their first chance to greet their boy. It was magic! Tears and tears and more tears. Amazement at his ears, at how he could eat, at his behaviour. It was obvious that they knew him well and cared for him. Then I read the card from Pat thanking them for allowing her to share their boy for a little while. Alosha's family promised to take him home and keep him as long as possible. Five months later he is still with them. There is something beautiful about him and about the hard-work love which brought him from a little bandy-legged boy in an empty green room where he sat with his forehead on the floor to now where he lives with his family, can feed himself and looks beautiful with his lovely blue eyes and blond head. Family is still the best place for children.

We miss him terribly.

Later, as we supported the family and their Alosha it became obvious that living on a fifth floor flat was unsuitable for him. It took too long to get him down the five flights of stairs as there was no lift. When he began to get upset, he needed to get outside quickly. He loved to sit and play on a swing. Kathleen and friends in Ennis decided to buy a groundfloor flat for Alosha and his family. They gathered their forces and their pennies and put together the required money to solve this child's greatest need. Alosha's granny is still speechless at the blessings that dropped from the sky into their lives, at the generosity that was borne from their handicapped boy, Alosha, group six, Cherven home for mentally and physically handicapped children. It is wonderful.

When Alosha was here he loved opening and listening to doors, he understood their talk, their squeaks. He sometimes found his way to our little chapel and went in there and sat down and rocked himself back and forth, his back to the door or towards the tabernacle. Rocking away. Quietly persistent.

It seems to have worked.

CHAPTER FIVE

Get up, take up your mat and walk

One of the hardest things to do emotionally is to let go of one child, let him return and almost lose touch with him and then concentrate on someone else. Our natural tendency was to stay with someone like Alosha and not have the Christian sense and toughness to move on to someone else. We had to treat each child as special, as individual, as having very special needs. But we also had to move quickly to where the need was greatest. Life doesn't happen in nice, neat, time-line packages. Everything is hurly-burly, all together. In the midst of it all, we sought out the ones most in need. The ones most in danger. Like the new little arrival in the orphanage.

Vika Veraskouskaya is the name of the little girl. She arrived into the orphanage while we were there one summer doing our usual round up of voluntary work. She was cute and pretty. We would have put her in a bag to bring her home! She was placed in group four, the unit for children who do not walk. Vika had come from a baby orphanage and obviously was well looked after and loved. She was beautiful. We hated leaving her there, as indeed it was hard to leave the place knowing that the children needed so much love and attention. It was impossible for the workers to provide that level of care amongst so many.

It was policy to shave off a child's hair and so Vika became a skinhead. We were so sad about this but could understand the hygiene needs of such a policy. It was only months later when we were back on our next trip that we saw the real change in her. It wasn't just her hair that had altered. Instead of a beautiful little girl she looked like a wizened little monkey, her face old and lacking all the beauty we remembered. Her stomach was distended, swollen out like the picture of the poor children we used see from Biafra. She was skinny and weak. We couldn't understand how such a change could come about in such a short time.

There were rumours that this unit was not properly fed in order to reduce the amount of changing of 'nappies' and in order to prevent the children from becoming large and heavy. On seeing Vika we began to think that maybe these rumours were true. But maybe it was simply that the food was not good enough. Or that she did not like it. Or maybe there was a medical reason for her condition.

That summer we were back again working with the children and increasingly concerned about the state of Vika. We knew she should be able to walk but was left all day in a bed. We had seen how healthy she had been when she arrived to the orphanage and now she was becoming emaciated and swollen. It had to be malnourishment and total lack of care. Little Sergei was in this same unit. The doctor told us, 'It is her disease.' But he has no treatment, no medicine, no special care. He has nothing to treat her with even if he wanted to. It is important to understand that in Belarus at this time there is a serious problem in the hospital and health care services. If you need to go to hospital, you must bring all your requirements. That includes syringes, drip, bandages, etc. You then need to pay the doctors and nurses to ensure you get looked after. There is no point in sending a handicapped orphan to hospital. It will be no better for them there. Our only hope was to bring Vika to Ireland and hope to care for her here. It was then that Kevin and Anne said they would look after her in Liscannor. So they took her home.

'I've never in my life come across a child in such a state of malnourishment. In terms of statistics of children's weight she is off the bottom of the page. She doesn't even register. She needs immediate treatment and long term hospital care. She has not long to live.'

Thank God for Dr Mahony, Sister Pat and the staff of the Regional Hospital in Limerick. The treatment began. We didn't know how long it would take, how successful it would be, whether we could afford it, or what the eventual outcome would be. We only knew we had to do something and this was it.

Bit by bit, ounce by ounce, Vika came back. 'I'll take her home with me,' said Anne 'when she's all right again. She's coming with me. I've the cot ready. And lovely clothes. She's coming to my place. She's mine.' It was almost a competition with all the many mothers of sick children who called in to see the little girl, Vika. They all loved her and would have willingly taken her home. But Anne was Mamma. And that's all there was to it.

One day I visited the hospital with Anne. Vika was on the floor trying to take off her clothes. She loved stripping off all her clothes. I picked her up and stood her up in front of me. Anne was sitting on a chair opposite. Anne called to Vika. 'Here, Vika. Come to Mamma.' Vika took her first step. Then another. Anne caught her. Anne looked at me. I looked at Anne. I had never actually seen the first step of a child. Did you see that? Did you? Did it happen? We both laughed. It was brilliant. Brilliant that she had taken her first step. But also the implications! This wasn't just a first step, but it was the first step to normality. The first step away from being left in a bed all her life. It meant she would be mobile, she would move. She would get out of group four where children are always left in bed. Even some who can walk have been left in bed so long that they have lost the use of their legs. Now, Vika was free from that. She was on her way to a better life. Simply by taking her first step in the Children's Ark in the Regional Hospital in Limerick. Brilliant!

Later when it was time to go, we said our goodbyes. I then said, 'Paka' which is goodbye in Russian. Vika repeated 'Paka'. Again we looked at each other. Did you hear that? Yes, did you? Did Vika say 'Paka'? Yes! Walking and talking on the same day. It was one of those very magical moments – twice. In one day!

Vika was very cute. But she was also quite difficult. She needed time and lots of energy. Slowly she began to make progress. Anne taught her 'Walkie round the garden' and to bless herself. Kevin played with her every evening and really loved her. She got to know the family members as well as Patch, the family dog. Then, eventually the time came for the big decision. Would she stay or would she go back to the orphanage? It was a difficult time. Work commitments meant that Anne could not give Vika the time she needed. I felt that now that Vika was on the way to recovery, we should concentrate on the ones who would die. Two had already died in group four and it was a source of great regret to us that we had not got to them in time. Perhaps if Vika went back and the workers saw how she improved with proper care, they might look after the others better. Maybe they would. Maybe they wouldn't. Maybe we could get Vika into a better group? After all now she was walking and should not be put back in a bed and left there. There was no need for it. The debate went on. Many tears flowed, especially at the end of the six month stay in Ireland and eventually we accepted the hard-made decision to let her go back for now, with the promise of keeping a close eye on things. We would be out there again in a couple of months and then she could come back over the winter.

Off we went. I travelled with them again to see how they would settle back. Alosha was also going back and also blind Sergei. The flight from Shannon to Minsk was fine. We were met by the orphanage minibus at the airport and headed for Cherven. We drove in the compound gates and dropped Alosha into group six. He would stay here until we contacted his family. Then they took Vika to group four. I stayed with Alosha to see his reaction to being back in his group. Then I followed to group four. Sergei was back in his bed, hands behind his head, relaxed and looking at home. Vika was back in the same bed inside the door, blanket up over her head asleep. In the morning we would see about moving her.

It was Saturday. Certainly she would be moved. But better wait until the proper rota of staff in group eleven came in on Monday. By now Vika was back in her old curtain-material *pilonka*/nappy thing, her lovely new clothes were nowhere to be seen and as we passed she reached up, pleading to be taken out of the bed.

On Monday morning we had to leave early to get to our second orphanage and make a beginning there. We trusted the assurances that Vika would be moved and off we went to Goradishche. This is also another story, of which again more later. Three days later we were on our way back to Minsk in Boris's ambulance preparing for our return home. We needed to make a call to customs control at the airport as apparently some of our Humanitarian Aid shipments were being opened and pilfered by the customs workers. No luck solving that problem as it was lunch break. Maybe they saw us coming! We had a little time to spare and Lisa, our secretary who was travelling with us, in her wisdom suggested that it might be a good idea to make a quick unscheduled trip to Cherven just to make sure, for certain, that our wishes had been carried out.

We entered the compound quickly and without the usual formalities of meeting director or his delegate, we headed straight for group four. There was Vika in her bed inside the door, hands up in the air pleading to be taken up. Blind Sergei was in his bed dirty and wet, wet up his back, on his pillow, everywhere. Further along, big Alosha to whom we had given a little walkman as he is very unwell, was without his gift. It had been taken from him by one of the workers. We were mad! Nothing of our wishes had been done. We had failed the children. After all the hard work, the hospital care, the expense, the loving kindness that these children had received in Ireland! Now, only this. As though it didn't matter! As though we had wasted our time! As though it was all a joke! Only for the quiet, insistent voice of Lisa once more, we would have gone home presuming that everything was as it should be.

We demanded explanations. We demanded answers. We demanded that Vika be moved – now! as we had been promised. We demanded that Alosha get his player back and condemned the system where a drunken worker would steal from an invalid, dying child. We insisted that Vika be moved now. And why was Sergei left dirty and wet? Who was in charge? Where is the head nurse? Who is responsible? Vika couldn't be moved because the doctor wouldn't sign the papers. It would happen on the first of the month. It would happen on Monday. It was too dark ... or too bright ... or there was a full moon ... or no r in the month! Then, it could happen. Let's see the doctor. He signed the papers. Is there a problem in the other group? No. So, let's bring her there now. So we did. Where are her clothes? We don't know. The person in charge is off! And so it went! Eventually, Vika was moved to a unit where she would be up and about, where there was some attempt to stimulate and provide learning for the children. But why do we need to get mad to bring about such obvious changes? There must be something about the system here that we simply do not understand! Why are there not better conditions, better facilities for the children? How can the workers possibly cope in these situations?

Two months later Anne went to visit for herself. To see how Vika was doing. We had taken measures to ensure we would know if there was any deterioration in her condition. Anne was delighted to meet Vika. Vika was delighted to meet Anne. She did her 'walkie round the garden' and blessed herself and barked like Patch all at the same time.

Now we are planning again and Vika will come again to spend more time with Anne and her family. Group Eleven have been wonderful and have toilet-trained Vika and really helped her in many, many ways. Thank God for her first step and for the chance she got to walk, to get out of her bed and begin to have some sort of quality of life. She even knows some of the letters of the Russian alphabet. She will continue to be part of our lives and very much part of Anne and Kevin's family. We will not lose touch.

Group Eleven, where Vika now lives, is a swarm of gorgeous Down's Syndrome children and is full of energy and love. We live and hope that together we can make things much better for so many more. Because always we think, what about all the others? Luda who works there in group eleven has a great love for these children and for Vika. She told me that when Vika hears or sees an aeroplane flying over in the sky, she waves her hand and says 'Mamma Anne'. She has made contact. She knows where they are. They are in her heart also.

CHAPTER SIX

Those who are healthy don't need a doctor

Sometimes life can backfire a little, especially when one is trying to be a little clever. We were a bit concerned about the rate of progress in Cherven Orphanage and thought it would be a good idea to have a second orphanage to play off against it, to say well, if ye don't get on with it we will move someplace else. So we sought out a second orphanage. As luck would have it, we also had had a call from Fr Brendan O'Donoghue of Shannon saying that his parish were willing to row in behind a new orphanage as their Millennium Project 2000 if we could find a suitable place in Belarus.

It was the week of the St Patrick's Day parade in Minsk, a beautiful clear sunny day; crisp, sparkling snow all round us as we paraded down Gorky Park in Minsk lead by Sonia on fiddle and the Kilkenny gang adding various accompaniments. The day was filled with crack and seminars, talk and chat, meetings and presentations. It was a very full day of getting to know each others' traditions and building better links for the future.

The following morning our trip to this new orphanage of Goradishche had been organised. It is only a couple of hours from Minsk and was on the way south-west. Boris in the ambulance got us there without any bother and we arrived into the compound. This place had an open gate which maybe meant things weren't as bad as elsewhere. The director met us, a laid-back middle aged man, showing possible signs of wear. Basically all we wanted was a quick trip around the place, visit the children, see if it was in need of help and get permission from the director to set up the Shannon link.

There are moments in life which stick with you for ever. There are images which refuse to disappear, and there are smells which haunt, bringing back in a vivid way a time or place or event. As we went down the corridor to the bed-victims, we got it. The smell. Urine. Dirt. Foul air. A stairs lead up to the right. In front a large door into Group 3, the beddies. A loud bang on the door and it was opened from the inside. It was too late to draw a breath of fresh air. We were already enclouded in the smell. We moved into the corridor. The smell was unbelievable! A little old lady from Denmark was inside the door. She spoke English and told us how she had come there to do something about the place and would spend two weeks trying to make a difference. She was an elderly lady who had seen something on television about the place and decided to try to do something about it. We moved on to see what we would see.

First room had fourteen handicapped people in cots. Four of my shoe-size long. The smells were foul. Flies crawled over the faces of the kids. How could anyone work here, not to mind live here? All the windows were closed as they were more afraid of the cold than any smells or infection. Marina had to leave. Ruslan apologised and left to go outside for fresh air. We went along to see the children. They just lie there in their various stages of handicap and abandonment. I think, Shannon, we got what you wanted! A place in need! There was just about room to move between the beds .

Natasha, a big girl all excited to see us, was one of the few to show some reaction. Little Valya looked out over the rails of her cot. Very sick children lay along by the wall. One child was projectile vomiting lying on his back behind the door.

In the middle beds, in the middle of the room were two brothers. A sort of net separated the two small beds. Sasha and Sidorzhe. Aged late teens, early twenties. Intelligent eyes looked up at us. Using my poor Russian I spoke to them and they responded. These obviously were as big as myself, pushing six foot tall, but cramped in small beds. I was mad.

'Why are these men in these small beds?' I asked in anger.

'That's all they need,' came the reply.

The anger burnt within me. But what to say? (A week later back in Ireland I could not keep food down. I was sick. It lasted until I realised that it wasn't sickness but the anger I swallowed in that room with those young men. Only then did my stomach settle). I was so mad! Here were these two fine young men confined to these small cots. We looked under the blankets. Their legs were bent up and twisted, of no use now. Even at this stage we insisted that these should have proper beds with room to move. (These were provided shortly afterwards.) But of what use?

Down the corridor we went and into each of the five small rooms. In each there were six severely handicapped and ill children. Some tried to lift themselves out of the beds when we touched them. The smell everywhere stank. The handicap was also severe, especially for us who had so little knowledge and awareness of this side of life. I seriously thought that if I had a packet of tablets that would let these children go off asleep to their Maker, then I would surely give them out. Anything would be better than existing in this stink, with so little care and with such handicap. As the food buckets arrived we moved on. The little Danish lady explained that she had tried to do something, tried to put in cleaning agents and scents but they were taken. She is some lady to try! She had had no food, she said, only what she could scrape together herself. We hadn't much with us but left her all we had.

'How do you look at these children?' asked our interpreter. It was not easy. Then on into Group 8. Unbelievable! This was like an ordinary kindergarten or playgroup. A lovely, colourful, happy, bright group of excited small children. Beautiful. But only down the other side of the corridor. How can this be the same place?

Out the back we visited the other groups. The crawlers. A large group of children, most of whom cannot walk, live their lives in an empty room where they sit all day. Beautiful Paulina, a lovely gypsy girl was here. She can walk and talk. She sang for us. A happy, cheerful, smiling song. In the middle of all this. She laughed and smiled. And later asked us for a doll. We will have it next time. For most of the people here, adults and children, crawlers and walkers, boredom stood like a giant in each room, etched across faces of children and workers like another commanding person in the place. Dirt and smells we could cope with and could remove. But the boredom, inactivity, no place to do anything – these would be bigger problems. We gave out sweets as we went, sometimes quietly, sometimes they were grabbed. Sometimes it was hard to see beyond the physical to the people and the lives that were lived here. Surely it was as difficult for the workers on twenty-five dollars a month as it was on the children, maybe even harder, as these children had never known anything else, had never been anywhere else and had no understanding of a different way of being.

I'm not sure about the others from Ireland, but for me, I didn't sleep properly for a month after this visit. All the time I kept seeing the intelligent faces of the young men in these groups and thinking what a horrid existence it must be. All we had done was look and see and then left them. That very night we were back in Minsk watching a wonderful performance of Swan Lake with full orchestra in a lavish production in the gilted Opera House bathed in soft chandelier light. I was back in Goradishche with my boys in Group three, in the smells and the flies. This is surely a different world, another time warp!

It was only later after many visits that Irina, our interpreter, pointed out to us how the children react when we arrive. The first question is always, 'How long are your staying?' They want to know how many days we will be in the place. How many days excitement they can look forward to. For them, it is much more important than new toilets. It is much more important to have someone to sit with, someone who will put their arms about you, someone who will make you feel loved. As we have found out.

So began a several-pronged attack. First make sure the people of Shannon are aware of the situation. Time to wake them up to the reality of life for these children. Talks at Mass began in earnest. The priests, Fr O'Donoghue and Fr Tom Ryan, pushed things along greatly. All kinds of ideas were begun to raise money. There would be a collection every two months. OK! What else? Instead of a flower wreath at a funeral, people could make a donation to the cause in the deceased person's name. Instead of a Mother's Day wreath, or Father's Day one, a donation could be made and a certificate presented to the person instead. Confirmation and Communion children were encouraged to make a contribution to a child who would not have such chances. Golf people rowed in and held a classic. A little lady working in a hotel gathered up the used soaps and put them together for us. This was vital. Several young ladies ran a spon-

sored Dublin City Mini-Marathon. A céilí was held in Davy
Fitzgerald's place. People donated clothes, toys and wheelchairs.
The rumble began.

Meanwhile, in Fanore Brid Queally and John were planning
to raise a few pounds at their stables. A sponsored horse-hack
through the beautiful Burren should be attractive. And so it
proved to be with over one hundred and eleven horses turning
up to take part and provide a huge amount of money to the
cause. It was a brilliant and beautiful day as the horses made
their way from Fanore over the Burren to finish up with a feed in
Doolin. Experienced and inexperienced, young and old, turned
up to help out and to take part in this mighty effort. It was wonderful. And we have wonderful photos of eighty-five year old
Mrs Barrett making sure that local priest Fr Michael Reilly had a
good rub down after enduring the horseride over the Burren.
Don't know how she treated his saddle sores!

All the while we were packing boxes of soap, shampoo,
clothes, toys, games and sending them by air to Minsk where
they were then shipped to Goradishche. Panadol by the thousand, toothbrushes, toothpaste, more soap and loads and loads
of clothes. Boxed, packed and sent in the hope that it would
make a difference. It didn't at this stage, as they gave it away.
Yes, the director gave it away. What is the point in giving jeans
to these children in bed? What is the point in giving them new
clothes? We cannot give it to them because they can have only
three t-shirts. Here we were up against it again! We cannot … It
is not allowed … We cannot burn the old ones as the inspector
will ask where are they … And really we don't care a lot about
these children anyway, seemed to be the attitude. No one does.

It is easy to change beds but again so hard to change attitudes. If you keep the children clean it will be easier and more
pleasant for yourself. So hard to change attitudes. But we kept at
it. In July, we flew out again and six of us headed for
Goradishche. We would spend a few days with the children and
see what we could do to make a more lasting difference. We
began with the bed children. We really wanted to get as many as
possible up and out, cleaned and washed. Where to begin?

Anywhere! So we began. We lifted big Sasha out of the bed,
his useless legs fell down from his body and the sores at his

joints opened. His eyes moisted in pain. We brought him to the
table, scraped the dirt off his back, cleaned him, massaged him
all over, cut his toe-nails and put new clothes on him. His bed
was changed while he was out of it. Then on to Sidorzhe. Same
routine. Clean, wash, scrape the dirt off, oil up and massage,
sudocream on the bedsores, slap it on, toes, fingers and new
clothes. Pat and Neilus, Triona and Tommy, Bid and myself
worked our way through the forty-four handicapped bed-rid-
den children and young people in Unit Three. I nearly puked at
the belly buttons. Bums I could manage. Twisted, in-grown nails
I could cope with. Twisted limbs, dirt, no problem. But belly
buttons … yuck! 'Bid, I'm going to be sick. What will I do with
the belly button?' 'Squeeze a little oil in, get a cotton bud. There
you're doing fine!' And on we went.

It took three days to get round to everyone. The smell of the
place was much improved … or were we just accustomed to it?
It was surely better. We were getting to know these people as we
worked, their personalities as well as their conditions. Some of
them were just gorgeous. Others had disappeared into themselves. The loss of human contact had made them less human.
Their souls were somewhere out there on the fringes of space,
only barely still linking with the body of these children. There
had been no-one to hug the body and soul together, no one to
mould together the spirit and body, and so the unity was falling
apart, the soul was drifting away, the spirit no longer at home in
a body which no-one loved. It is a great insight into how we
need human touch, how we need to be needed, to be known as
ourselves, to have a valued identity, to be someone in the eyes of
someone else. And even when it was not easy, we went and
made contact, we touched and held, we massaged and stroked.
Stroked the spirit, coaxed the soul back into the body, tried to
encourage the life to come again, in the heart and in the mind
and in the completeness of the unity of the person. As their bodies sprawled over the bed, it seemed too that their spirit also
sprawled and drifted to the edges. We begin to realise that the
most important part of all our work is the sheer human contact,
the picking up, the tickling, the loving human contact. It is this
which heals, this contact which brings a person back together
again. And I remember a guy begging in Dublin years ago and

he cried, 'No body gives me anything, ' and now I wish I had been the one to give something to him and now I know that here I have the chance to give something as simple as human touch and contact and it will make a difference to them and to me. I do not go unmoved by meeting the souls of these precious angels. It is they who are putting me back together again, in this Humpty-Dumpty land, making contact with the vital of life, the really important. But it is not easy sometimes. And there are some hard to pick up and say 'I love you' to. But sure we can only try. And who knows but that the Great Spirit, Master of the Universe, has the same difficulty or the same joy in picking each of us unto itself.

This is the task ahead, this is the job we have now landed ourselves with. To let all these children know that we love them. To bring a little joy and happiness into their lives. And to keep on doing it! How will we make out? How will we manage? Who will survive the trip? Can we make a real difference to the lives of the unwanted? We will try. That is our commitment. To be there for these children. To bring a little love into their lives. To give them something to hope for, something to look forward to. They know that we will be back. They know we will bring bananas and yogurts. They know we love them. We will try to hold them all in our hearts and in our hands. Not just as a symbol but in a real hands-on way. Buy Paulina her doll. Get Sasha his player. Tickle Vitalic back to laughter. Bring them back from the edges. Bring us back from the brink of forgetting important things. We will sow love. Because for so many of the children, whatever their state of being, the question they ask is, do you love me, will you be my pappa, will you be my mamma? And we will. In English. In Russian. In any language. We will love and be loved.

Ya loobloo tebya! I love you.

CHAPTER SEVEN

This is your mother. This is your son

It can only be the grace of God which has brought Teresa and Sergei together. From time immemorial the cry of Sergei has been echoing through the cosmos. He arrived to Cherven Orphanage in January 1999 in a state of total malnourishment. Teresa was there in February for a short visit and remembers seeing him. When we went out again to work there in June he was still alive. He couldn't eat or drink. He was getting no food or care which he needed. Eileen began working on him with Pat and they succeeded in getting some milk and in getting it into him. They began to try to squeeze aloe vera jel into his mouth to try to heal the ulcers on the back of his throat. He was in total spasm, every cell of his body on the brink of decay and death. As we left the orphanage that summer it was Sinead who said: 'What are you going to do about Vika? What about Sergei?' It was only then I realised that we had to do something more.

It was October 1st when we got Sergei to Ireland. He was still alive but could have died on the aeroplane. At five and a half years, he weighed seven kilos. Yes, that is about fifteen pounds weight. At five and a half years. We were afraid to touch him. Afraid to leave him alone.

Teresa said she would take him home. And so she did. They have been in continuous soul-dialogue since then. The cry from eternity has been echoed. A crucified cry. A total response. Elizabeth in her old-age. Only the very precious souls come in severely handicapped bodies. Only the very special souls recognise this. In Teresa and Sergei there is inspiration for us all. There is complete acceptance and love. And communication at a special level.

Out of the depths

I remember him in group four, a little shape in a large bed, monkey hairs over his little face and body, barely there at all. I remember the flies on his face and, of course, he hadn't the strength to brush them away. I didn't know his name or anything about him, where he was from, who he was. But I knew him in my heart.

I don't remember when you came. I don't recall your voice. Sometimes noise around me, sometimes a big spoon stuck in my mouth, I tried to grasp it, to hold on, to feed myself this way. They pulled it from my mouth. The spoon passed on … someplace else.

Twenty four or five little ones in this ward, all in need of food and cleanliness and love, the workers themselves not much better and with just as little joy in some of their lives.

Five years crucified, holding on, months gasping, holding on to life. My throat dried up from nothing passing it, my body like a dried up grape, each day I am descending, becoming less, fading away and no-one cares. I cannot call, I cannot scream, I cannot cry for help. My only hope that in my disappearing someone will finally notice. That someone will be a mother to me.

You are five years of age, only about ten pounds weight. You cannot even suck a bottle. There are ulcers on the back of your throat. Trying to squeeze aloe vera gel into your little mouth to help ease the soreness. We have located milk and a bottle and are trying to teach you to suck. He doesn't want to eat, say the workers. I hear your cry saying that I will walk away too like all the others. That I will leave you here too, abandoned and forgotten. I hear you.

I notice something different. People about me. My mouth hurts but there is something to eat. I cannot do it well. I want to. I want to help you help me but my body, my mind don't work well. I try to grasp the spoon, the bottle … please don't give up on me yet. I will come back from the brink.

Only the very special souls choose to come to life in these bodies. Only those great souls choose to spend their earth time in the body of a severely handicapped child. They are the very special ones, the very special souls. Sergei is a beautiful child, with a very beautiful soul.

It is October and I am moving. Something different. Going someplace. Maybe this is the end. Others have died here and disappeared. A plane ride, a new place, a new bed. Something different. Hard to see or understand. Even my eyes don't work properly now as hunger has its awful effect. Is this what it's like to be five?

Jesus! Christ Almighty! He is five and a half years, he is fifteen pounds weight. He cannot suck. His head is held back in pain. The little angel. He is too sick for hospital. They will want blood samples and tests and needles stuck in him. And crowds around him. Sure we can't have that. I will take the little angel home with me. Before the other crowd of orphans arrive. It will be too noisy, too rough for him here. I'll take him to my place. Give him here to me.

This place is different. Different lights, heat. People more often coming to me. I like it here. Soft music, flickering home-fire. It's not group four. Mamma?

The little angel, he is beau-ti-ful. The little darling. He loves Deepak Shopra music. It is healing music, very good. The little angel, sure he is all dried up, nothing of his body works, how could it? It has been deprived of all nourishment for so long. It will take a long time to come back. Sure every organ, every cell of his body is in need of healing. It will all take time. And sure we have plenty of that.

Thank you for the milk, and the milk with honey, and the love, and the everyday beautiful smile telling me I am beautiful. I want to live now too.

Oh! I am so excited, this morning at two o'clock we had a dirty nappy. Very small, mind you, like little pebbles, but still … it is the beginning. Sure his entire system must be dried up, out of order, the little angel. He is so beautiful!

It hurts, coming back hurts. Pains and aches as I begin to function again. I wonder can I make it back. Teresa will make it happen. She smiles and loves me all the time. I know this. In my way. I want to say things, to say thanks, to reach out. Believe me, I am trying. I try. In the darkness, in the night, I try to practice sounds, to make sense of what I hear, to place together the bits and pieces, the smiles and sounds, to try to respond. Here, in the darkness I try. Kick my legs and try to make this mind work, to bring it back to life, to talk with you, to send you stars of light.

They say his mother is in jail. He suffered trauma of the brain at one month and is this way as a result. Maybe he was dropped or kicked or abused in some way, the little angel. The doctors say he won't ever walk, but we'll see ... sure what do they know about it, really? We must always expect miracles. Every day miracles all round us. Who is to know? He is so beautiful!

Massage is nice. I like to kick my legs. The left one doesn't work so well yet but it is so nice to lie on the bed and kick. I like to laugh and smile and to be rattled. I am coming back to life. I want to laugh and chortle, to giggle and to hear the wonder of my own voice. What a noise, what a wonderful noise. I can make sounds.

As he grows, scars and marks appear on his body. Of course, when he was so small and deprived of nourishment there was no way we could see them but now as his flesh fills out we see the little burn marks and the scars which show what he suffered. The little angel, he is so beautiful.

I don't like some of those drinks. Bitter and not nice.

Oh thank God the little angel is beginning to spit out the stuff. He is beginning to know the difference, to show what he wants and what he doesn't like. And a wonderful nappy last night .I changed him at two o'clock and then he slept the night long. Isn't he beautiful!

Thank you Teresa, for minding me. For taking me into your home, and into your bed where I could sleep in comfort with the heat of your body and the love of your heart all about me. I love the stars on your ceiling and the wondrous joy of waking up each morning. I am glad you are not a morning person.

Ya loobloo tibya. I love you.

Every day, I thank the Lord for the wonder of your being.

In the name of the Father and the Son and the Holy Spirit. Amen.

We were frightened that Sergei would not make the trip, the trip from Belarus to Ennistymon and indeed the trip back to health. But he is making it, he is on the way. Teaching us all, loving us all and reminding us all of things we had forgotten in our busyness. He may never walk or talk. But now he laughs – and how we rejoice on hearing his beautiful gurgle of a laugh. You can see the amazement and joy in his own face as he experiences the sensation of laughter. All it takes is a little shake and he lights up, smiles and gurgles in joy. It is a wondrous sound.

Now he has trebled his weight. A long way from the early days when we tiptoed into the room to see if he was still alive. A longer distance from the time when he did not sleep for three days such was his state of deprivation. And then he slept. And then we dared hope that this was the first sign that he would make it back. Healing sleep. Deep, healing sleep. And the hope that there would come life again. And we worried that we weren't lifting him correctly, or that he wasn't comfortable. And then we realised the struggle and the strength of the little fifteen-pound five-and-a-half year old and knew that he was a real fighter, and if he could survive months of the starvation and neglect that he had been through, then he would fight on and live, when surrounded with a little love, milk and honey and the homefires of Teresa's house and heart.

And how much he has taught us all, how much he has given to each and every one who has seen him, who has seen where he has come from and how he now lies in sleek contentment waiting only to be loved and to love. And he is loved, the little angel.

CHAPTER EIGHT

He took her hand and helped her up

Sergei's mother is in jail for murder. Of course, Sergei could never say it, but we knew he wanted us to help her and the other two thousand five hundred women in that jail in Gomel Prison, southeast Belarus. We had sent from Ireland two lorries of humanitarian aid. These had arrived in Minsk. It would take a while to get customs documents sorted but even this situation has improved of late. Maura and I had flown out after the lorries to ensure that everything was done as it should be and that the goods arrived where we wanted them to go. On the Monday evening we met up with the drivers Liam Grant and Tony Quirke to have a drink to celebrate their arrival with the new toilets and shower units which we had planned to install in Cherven orphanage. These two lorry loads of humanitarian aid would make a real difference to the lives of the children. Later that night, walking home through the quiet of the Minsk city street, my mind was on the following day's journey. It was to be the day we would visit the jail in Gomel and hopefully meet Teresa's Sergei's mother. I had never visited a jail before, not even in Ireland and here I was now about to visit a jail in the former Soviet state of Belarus. It is a long way from Ennistymon and a longer way from my own small place of Bohercarron.

Boris, our driver, picked us up at eight thirty the following morning. Maria was with us as interpreter. The four-hour journey was quiet as we focused on what lay ahead. We weren't even sure we would be allowed access. We went on a hope and a prayer and the candle which Teresa had alight back home in Freagh Castle. Gomel is the second city of Belarus but is in no way cosmopolitan or European in its daily bustle. We found it almost impossible to find something to eat and equally difficult to find a toilet but that was nothing new to us. We queued up with all the lovers, wives and mothers at what we thought was the jail and were informed that we were in the wrong place. This was merely where alleged criminals were held before trial. One lady roared out a stream of Russian at us as we had apparently not joined the queue properly. So back across town to try to find the right prison.

In all Belarus and the former Soviet states there is a great presence of various Militia and police-uniformed people. Entering a prison would be especially daunting. Would we even get out again? From the outside it didn't look too terrible. The tall fence and high wall were to be expected. The blond-dyed lady at the gate fitted in with the usual, her pet rat asleep in the flower pot on the table in her hut. She loved the idea of having her photo taken with us and was delighted to get some cigarettes. We walked on down the yard and came to a small door with a bell. Out through this door came barging the Prison guards coming off duty or to outside work. These guards were tough and hard looking, and as the joke goes, the men were even worse. Some male wardens arrived also and began various horseplay with some of the women. Nothing very outrageous but it made us wonder that if this is the way they behave among themselves what will it be like for the women prisoners inside. Perhaps an unfair thought but it passed through our minds.

We were allowed in the door with the bell after several rings. Behind a glass window a faceless uniformed man was in control. He held a rope in his right hand which was pulled to open the door to allow people in or out. Several more staff passed through and he would open the gate only when they responded properly to his approaches. It added to the intimidation of the place that we might have to grovel our way back out. And yet I felt we were on a mission and would succeed. Maria explained what we were about. Eventually a beautiful stone-maiden, nothing being given away in her face, arrived, to meet us. Maria explained about our work with the orphanages, about all the help we give, about having Sergei in Ireland and we would like to see his mother. No chink! I took out the photos of Sergei when he was starving and showed them to her. A beautiful woman like her must have children and might understand. She asked for our passports but this was another problem in this country. Our passports were in the hotel as we had to hand them over on arrival. Boris and Maria handed over theirs now and our lady-friend went off outside to some other place. We watched the antics and horse-acting of the prison guards outside the small window. We waited quietly and in hope that we would be successful.

She came back. Again her face unyielding but not in any way unfriendly. The face behind the glass called out Boris's surname and Boris answered his name and patronymic. Then Maria's surname 'Mitskevich', to which Maria replied 'Maria Mikhail-ovna'. Like rollcall in school. To the right there was a door. We were allowed through. It crashed behind us. In front another door. We went through and this was closed behind us. We were now in the open with ten foot fencing on both sides of us. We headed straight through the opening ahead of us into a large courtyard. A three-storey building, brick, just like the orphanages. The yard was clean and orderly. Clumps of long-legged flowers swayed slightly in the centre beds. We veered to the right.

Eyes from under brows and behind upstairs windows squinted out to us. We had no means of reply. No way to penetrate the building and the barbed-wire-wrapped stories of the people behind the walls. The unseen, the unclean, the unknown, the unwanted. Small clusters of two, three or four women stood about, slowly attending to their duties. I tried to see into their eyes, into their hearts, into their stories. Two ladies emerged from a door on our left and stood to look at us. Our lady director sharpened out a question about whether they had work to do and they snapped to.

I decided in the excitement of being inside the place to try a little charm with this lady.

'Do you work here a long time?'

'Yes.'

'It is difficult work?'

'Yes.'

And on we paraded through the yard towards a door in the opposite wall. Up a stairs to the right. Through a short, dark corridor and we were in the governor's office. He was grand! From behind his table, he extended a warm welcome to us and so began a long chat. Again the explanations of who we were and why we had come. Would it be possible to see this woman, mother of Sergei? Would it be possible to come back later with Sergei and Teresa to meet her. We spent some time discussing the difficulties of prison life, the lack of basic necessities. He had no shoes for the women even when they were released. No soaps and washing powder. No toiletries and hygiene products for the women. To me he seemed a warm type. A good man.

Then he asked where would we like to meet this woman. We didn't mind and suddenly there she was. We hardly realised it. It happened so fast. One minute she wasn't there. The next, she was. I got up to look. Was this her? Is this Sergei's mother? Did she look like him? It took only a few seconds I'm sure but it was an age. So many things rushing through my head. Only then did I realise how absolutely terrified she was. Shivering! Like a little brown sparrow with broken wings about to be pounced on by a cat. She stood there shaking. I went to embrace her. To tell her who we were. To put her at ease. We brought her to the side of the room to talk and to show her the photographs of her son, her beautiful son. In her fear she did not see them at first. Later we were able to think that maybe she didn't know we were there, maybe they just said get over now to the governor's office, maybe it is a desperate thing to be called to the governor's office when one is in prison. But we only realised that later.

We sat. Maura on her right. Maria in front. I hunched on the floor beside her. The lady from the prison sat where she could see everything and make sure that we were not passing on anything illegal or contraband. Sweets? We talked of how we love Sergei. Of how Teresa loves him to bits. Of how beautiful he is. Of how well he is doing. She asked about him. Was he big? Could he walk? Or talk? No but we love him all the more. Does he have any words? No, but he has beautiful sounds. We showed the pictures again. The bad one when he first came. This is Sergei? She couldn't believe it. She hadn't seen him in two and a half years. What had happened to him? She couldn't cope with this. Could any mother? So we brought out the beautiful photos of Sergei and Teresa, of how he is now. And she sat there and rubbed noses with the nose of her son in the photo.

And Teresa sat at home in her little house with a candle lighting, sending positive energy and love so that all would go well for the little angel. And all the while sitting there in the jail, I was absorbed with the awareness that it was Sergei who was now looking after his mother. It was his soul energy which was wrapped about us. It was he who had called out to us with his last efforts. It was he who had lead us here to this prison. It was he who was looking after her. It felt as though we had actually been led to the orphanage in Cherven in order to find him – led by his emanating energy – so that we would then be in a position to go to the jail and help his mother. The ultimate sacrifice. It was Sergei who was seeing to it that his mother was looked after, because we could not refuse this child anything. Indeed, he would be responsible for our trying to do something to help all two thousand five hundred and forty three women and their sixty three prison babies. It was Sergei in his handicap and in-ability who had brought us to this point.

So we told her again about Sergei and his massage with Marie and his physiotherapy with Christina and his visits to Galway each week to the beautiful chiropractor, Mr Bludworth. And we told how he loves to wake up in the morning and shrieks with delight at the new day. Every day. And we tried to remember all the little things. How he smiles . And laughs. And how he has terrible tickles. And she said that so has she. And I asked her about his past and she told us what she knew and her worries about him and searching from the prison for him and her fear when she heard he was in Ireland and not knowing what might be happening to him and the relief in knowing he was looked after. And I asked her how she was and I knew by the reply that not too many have asked that question of her in the past two years. But she is strong and is young and will make it back to a life in the village. God love her.

Too soon it was time to go. We stood up. She was told to say thanks. Like school. She said thanks. Hugs all round. And I gave her a hug and said it was from Teresa. And another hug. And told her it was from Sergei. We left her the photos and she disappeared down the yard. We caught a final glimpse of her back disappearing into the wire mesh on the right side, back to her quarters, her work, her space, no doubt to think, to cry, to rub noses again with the nose of her son in the photo.

We left presents and bits and pieces that might be needed

and took leave of the governor and the lady. Again I tried on our way back with this prison lady, I tried to find a chink, a way through but she held her composure and there was no way through to her heart.

The journey back to Minsk took four hours. It was a chance to sit and think about what had happened, to reflect and try to make sense of it all. I couldn't help being upset. It was such an emotional situation. The unfairness of our world sometimes really amazes me. Here we were with our bits and pieces, our small group, collecting money in buckets, fund-raising for pounds here and there to try and solve big problems. And I just felt ashamed of our world and yet amazed. Ashamed.

Ashamed that the real problems of the world, the world of physical and mental handicap, must be solved by elderly ladies in small cottages in the west of Ireland. By the likes of Teresa, a pensioner, willing to give of her time and her energy to love a fifteen pound five-and-a-half year old mentally and physically handicapped boy back to life. Ashamed of our social security system which would deprive her of six pounds a week living-alone allowance for taking this boy into her home. Of course, it was all returned one year later but this was the type of bureaucracy we met in Belarus and didn't expect to find at home.

But it is amazing how strong we each can be in our weakness. There is no power stronger than love, beautiful love. How unfair the world can be! And how wonderful when we decide to rely on the spirit of goodness of the universe. Only then is there sufficient to go around. And so I know that when next we bring a group of these children to Clare, they will be met by all the little people who feel they cannot do anything but who will turn up with love in money, in buns and cakes, in drives to the sea, to show that they too are part of the reality of love, in a real beautiful, quiet and gentle way. And this is what makes a real difference. So we head home again, this time to plan for the visit of Teresa and Sergei to see his mother in the prison in Gomel, in south-eastern Belarus.

CHAPTER NINE

Five loaves for five thousand
30 October 2000

Should we really take Sergei back to Belarus? Would there be some way to bring him back again – after just one week? Maybe they would not allow us to have him back? Perhaps they will want to do experiments to see how he has made such progress. Maybe they will simply refuse to allow him out again!

These were our thoughts as we began to plan the return trip with Sergei to visit his mother. Confident in the Lord that all would be well, we got ourselves organised. We started in Teresa's house in Freagh Castle. In this house Sergei had received love and attention over the past year and here he had recovered from being a fifteen pound five-and-a-half year old to one who was now about three stone and who was loved and cherished in a way that he needed in order to restore his health. Teresa had done this almost single-handedly over the past thirteen months and now we would take the big chance of returning to Belarus with him in the hope of meeting his mother, Natasha.

From my previous exploratory trip, we knew that she was in jail in Gomel and that she was there for allegedly murdering her brother. We didn't know the circumstances of that death but we knew that she was in jail for over two years and would remain there for another possible six. It had been Teresa's objective from the beginning that Sergei would be reunited with his mother if that was possible and that we should support her when she came out of jail. That might make possible a life for her with her child.

Mick Peelo as interviewer, together with the *Would You Believe* film crew, were travelling with us to record the trip for Irish Television. They had already done a programme on the work of the Burren Chernobyl Project earlier in the year and this had been very helpful in raising awareness and funds for the continuation of our work.

Filming began in Teresa's as we left and this in itself was strange. From now on, what we said and did would be under the eye of the cameraman. Many things would have to be repeated. 'Can you do that again please?' was a regular call from Breffni Byrne, cameraman. We knew that the journey ahead was emotional and we didn't know how we would react when each moment of our actions was being recorded. Packed and ready we headed for Shannon Airport. That particular Monday, 30 October 2000, there was a small crowd flying to Belarus. We had the plane to ourselves and were able to relax a little as we thought about what was ahead. The three-and-a half hour journey passed without incident and we arrived into Minsk International Airport, with Breffni in the cockpit filming the landing. New regulations meant that we had to fill insurance forms at the airport. The girls in charge of this business were in a dark corner of the airport and were trying to fill out the forms using a cigarette lighter. Breffni came to their aid with the use of his camera light. Through passport control without much trouble, then fill the customs declaration forms. We were used to this procedure by now but still found it a bother. The baggage workers knew us and came to offer their assistance with our luggage. They knew that we would tip with dollars and so were very cooperative. It did help considerably. There was a huge delay as the film crew had to list every last piece of their equipment twice over but eventually we did manage to get through and were greeted by Maria, Marina and Boris our driver. This was all filmed so we were again taking more time than normal. Delays are usual in Minsk airport and we were well used to not getting too excited about anything.

Pat O'Doherty went off with Fr Tom Ryan of Shannon as they were heading for Goradishche orphanage. Georgi, the director, had come to meet them and they were in the company of Irina the interpreter. We would meet up with them again later in the week, all going well. Already a group of men from Clare were ahead of us in Cherven Orphanage working on the installation of new showers and baths. They had travelled out the previous Friday. It would be a very busy week even with everything going according to plan. The rest of us went off to Minsk and checked into the Planeta Hotel. Luckily for us we were allowed stay at the local rate or else we could not afford to stay in such a place. It is a good place to stay as there is hot water and breakfast is served without having to order it in advance the night before as in some other places. Frances, who had been in Cherven Orphanage, came to join us in the hotel and so we had company and were able to be updated on the work in progress at the orphanage.

Later in the night we had a trip to the local McDonald's for a take-away while Teresa frantically tried to force her way into my locked suitcase for the electric kettle. Unfortunately I had the keys of the suitcase with me and so her craving for a coffee had to await our return with the burgers. We found her on her knees beating the floor in desperation.

Next morning was the day of days; the day we would go to the jail in Gomel and try to meet Sergei's mother in the hope that there would somehow be the possibility of her knowing her child whom she hadn't seen for over two years. It would give us an insight into how she felt about him. Many mothers and fathers in Belarus reject their child if they are in any way handicapped. They are officially entitled to do this at the birth of their child. Maybe it would be the same with Natasha? Or maybe it would be something she waited and hoped for every morning of her prison life? Today we would find out. We felt that both mother and child were entitled to the opportunity. I had already met Sergei's mother and carried the hope that all would be well. I felt this whole trip would somehow be well. All manner of things would be well.

Filming of the journey was part of the day's work and again took a little adjusting to. Filmed getting into the car, camera outside. Get out of the car and get in again, this time filmed from camera inside the car. Filmed from inside the car getting out. Then sit back into the car and get filmed from outside the car getting out. Where were your hands? Where was your scarf? We must have continuity! We coped fairly well generally with the instructions of producer, Margaret. Sergei was in command of his own situation and the four hour journey became five as he peed when he had to and, of course, drenched himself and his new clothes up to his neck to show that we might plan and organise but it was his day and he would do what suited him, like

it or not. As this situation had never happened in his previous
thirteen months with us, it did cause problems. There was now
only one set of clothes left for the journey. So much for a six year
old's bodily functions! It was late afternoon when the seemingly
endless journey finally brought us to Gomel. It is a beautiful
country to drive through, but endless. The jail was not too terribly prison-like from the outside, as I knew already, but a jail is a
jail. A prison is a prison. We were late. The Director patiently
put up with us and allowed us through and into the courtyard.
Again we would make our way across this yard to his office.
This was to be the meeting place, the place where a mother and
child apart for over two and a half years would meet up again.
Always the questions in our minds. Would she know him?
Would Sergei in anyway be able to say that he knew her or respond to her? Would we know by his reactions, sounds and
body language that the meeting meant anything – good or bad –
to him? Was it all a waste of time, energy and money? Or would
it be great? Would this be what moves the world? What life is
about? Would it be a special moment of love in which mother
and handicapped son came together in a loving embrace which
would blot out all obstacles and make a future possible? How
would Teresa react seeing the child to whom she had dedicated
the past year in a total and loving way now in the arms of his
real mother? Could she let go? Could she embrace this woman
in her fear and her torment and her prison-life and say 'Here is
your son'? Would it all be too emotional? How would any of us
cope?

Sergei's mother, Natasha, came in. Teresa handed him to her.
I sat and watched. Maria, our interpreter, waited. Perhaps only
mothers will know what it was like for a mother to arrive into a
prison office and be presented with her six year old whom she
hasn't seen for over two years. Only a woman's heart will know
what it meant for Teresa who has loved this child totally for the
past year, what it was like for her to hand her baby back to his
mother, in jail for committing murder. Only those who know
will understand the depth of the reaching out to this young girl
in jail and the powerful statement of trust, of acceptance, of
promise, of reassurance, from Teresa to her in handing Sergei
back into the hands of his mother. It is a statement of trust. It is a

huge statement of acceptance of another person as a person regardless of their circumstances. It is a huge act of selfless love to someone who has no choices. Teresa had the choice to visit or not to visit, to bring the child or not; to risk returning to Belarus with him without ever really knowing whether we would be allowed to bring him back to Ireland with us or not. It was a huge, huge generosity. One the world needs.

It is a situation which could have gone wrong. Mother might have rejected her child again and not cared. Thankfully she, of course, recognised him and wanted him and showed all the love which any mother will show for her long lost son. Natasha wept, Teresa wept, we all wept. And only Sergei rejoiced in the attention and, perhaps in his own way, aware that he had brought all the loving people in his life here together in this room at the back end of Belarus in a moment so special that we would take a long time to really understand the depth of it all. It was Sergei brought us together. It was because of him that there was any contact between us. Through him, his mother and all the other two and a half thousand women in that jail and their sixty-three prison babies would receive help from our friends in Ireland. And yet he cannot walk, he cannot speak, he cannot call to us. Our lives revolve around him and he leads us to draw deeply from the strengths and the powers scripted within us.

We spent some time with Natasha and then she had time with her son. Some of it was filmed and then there was quiet time for mother and child and Teresa to be together. It had been a long day. We were all exhausted. For Teresa, it was the hardest day of her almost seventy years, she said. It was tough. Physically, emotionally, spiritually. We had drawn on all energies to help us cope with the trip. It was a beginning, not an end. Time now to find a hotel and rest in Gomel for the night. We would come back tomorrow and have a little more time with Natasha, see some more of the jail and get a feel of the place. It was good to have a second meeting to look forward to. But it didn't help Teresa sleep that night. There was too much to think about, to store up for another time, to hold on to as the night approached. Holding on to Sergei in a hotel room as his mother cried herself to sleep, down town, across the road, in a prison cell.

We hadn't planned to stay overnight in Gomel but filming required more time the next day so we had to adjust our plans. Wear the same clothes tomorrow – for continuity – was our instruction. Sergei was restless and didn't sleep until late in the night. In the lobby of the hotel there were many girls looking for business. In the lobby there were many clients ready to avail of any possible offers. On the steps outside the hotel entrance there were some street children. I went out to meet them. Some years ago I had been here for a short visit and the children of the street hung around the hotel in the hope of getting money, food or some support. Vova was there. He sleeps in the furnace at the back of the hotel. It is warm there. He is nine. His parents are dead. There is no point in going home. His friend, Oxana, is twelve. Her mother was killed in a car crash. She does not cry but tells me about it simply. There is nothing to go home for but she will sleep at home, she says. I wonder how long before she is caught up in the inevitable street business now being conducted inside the hotel, even as we speak. I tell her where I am from and why we have come to Belarus, to help children, to bring them to Ireland. She says simply: 'Bring me.' Simply. Like a child. 'Bring me.' I ask what they need and they ask for food. I'm not sure where to get something for them so I give them money, about five dollars. They eagerly plan what to buy. There is a place in the hotel but they are not allowed in due to their appearance. So they disappear off somewhere else. Maybe they will be there again next time I go to Gomel. Maybe not.

Next morning arrives. Teresa has hardly slept. Late in the night, Sergei slept well. We go again to the prison and do some filming. Then we tour around to see life inside. There are so many women. In twos, in groups, tied up bundles going about their lives in jail in Gomel. The baby section is good, better than what we have seen in the orphanages for the handicapped. I ask the Director if he would come to be director of our orphanage. Teresa and Natasha are using the time to be together and to share Sergei. It is cold. We are outside in the prison compound but together. Huddled, sheltering by a wall, Teresa shows the photos of Sergei she brought and the locks from his first haircut which Tommy did back in Ireland. Natasha looks at them, tired-eyed. She didn't sleep last night either. Too many things in her head, she said.

It is time to go. Natasha hands back her son to Teresa. Gestures returned in their significance. There is no big scene. It is time to go. Time to say goodbye. We say our goodbyes and go. Natasha sees us off through the prison inner gate. We turn to let her see Sergei one last time. Teresa has promised to come again with him. There is trust and acceptance and knowing that all will be well. But we have to deal with it all yet. Now we leave. Thanks to the prison people. Then off on the long journey to the village where Sergei lived. We go now to meet Natasha's mother, Sergei's real Granny. To try to see what life for Sergei was like and would be like back in his village. A chance for Teresa to meet Sergei's people, granny, grandad and whoever else there might be.

The journey was endless. Not knowing where we were going added to the tedium. Somewhere along the way we stopped for a short break. Somewhere we stopped to change Sergei. Somewhere we stopped to use the green toilet facilities. At one stage we almost got lost taking a wrong turn. At another place, as we approached a village, a funeral was making its way towards us. Mourners followed the tree-festooned lorry bearing the corpse and close kin along the road. Death is the same in any language. Hearts break. Life must go on. Somewhere else we stopped to phone the orphanage. We needed to check on the work and to say we would not be arriving there today. But on we went through the day, sharing chocolate bars and sandwiches, into the evening and eventually arrived at the village. We were afraid of what we would meet. Many said it was a village of alcoholics. Family problems must lie ahead as we arrived from a foreign country into a poor village with what had been the starving child of a mother who had killed her brother. The complications were endless. Maybe we would not find the family. Maybe there would be an effort to keep the child there? Maybe they would not want anything to do with us? Maybe we had no business being there? But we felt the need to go there. We had to know if there was any possibility of Sergei having a future with his own people, in his own home village. We had to know if they knew the state he was in when we found him in the orphanage. This was the only way we knew how to find the answers to those questions.

Sergei's grandmother cleans out from pigs and looks after them. She earns five dollars a month. Grandad told us that he is a 'waiter' which means he waits all night in a place to make sure nobody steals from there. Sergei's uncle of seventeen years is about to begin work. They all drink. Uncle had the smell of it. Granny had the look of it. Grandad looked fairly sober. They live in extreme poverty. Let there be no blame if vodka is the one and only solace. But it is not an answer to any of the problems this country and these people are facing. They were delighted that we came. All dressed up and waiting for us to arrive. We were embraced and welcomed. They had even killed their pig for us. The extent of their open hospitality would make an Irish person wonder. Total acceptance into their poor household. They told us what they knew of Sergei's past. They hoped he would stay in Ireland where he would be properly looked after. We would surely hope so too as it would be impossible for any family on such low wages to raise a handicapped child.

We met Natasha's husband, not the father of Sergei, who is now with a new partner. Families can be so complicated. We met Sergei's half-brother, a beautiful blond, pale-faced child who sat beside Sergei and put his arm about his neck. We met auntie and we spoke with Natasha's brother. It is difficult to know what to do, what to say. A privilege to be allowed into the intimacies of a foreign family. So we sat and shared a eucharistic feast with these people, a feast of fresh pork, potatoes and some vodka and whiskey. Ourselves, the family and the television crew. Sergei's journey had again brought us further into his story. None of us knew where it would lead, let alone end. Now, we just sat and talked, sharing our stories, removing barriers of time, distance and language. All in the warm embrace of family together. All because of Sergei. A boy who doesn't walk or talk. A boy who never asks for anything. A boy just himself. It was Tony who later pointed out how handicapped children bring us through the barriers that divide us. The children get us to wait when we don't understand Russian. We don't give up in hopelessness. We stand and wait and try again to understand. Because it is a handicapped child who has brought us together, who makes the connection one to the other.

Later we were back in to the hotel, trying to settle, trying to rest. Trying to make sense and to draw out the answers. But it is impossible. As we sat in the hotel bar having a drink, a lady-of-the-night gave me a big slow wink. I asked Breffni for advice.

'Breffni, I've just been given a big slow wink. What should I do? Should I give you a hug?'

'Liam, don't hug me!'

Next day was the day we would return to the orphanage to see if there was any possibility of Sergei returning there. We already knew without question that this was not even a remote possibility. When we found Sergei here, he was less than fifteeen pounds weight. His return to live there would simply be a slow death sentence, death by starvation. We have made many trips to this orphanage. This time it seemed to me the children in many of the units were hungrier and skinnier and more starving than heretofore. It does our hearts no good to see this. Sergei's bed is occupied by Alosha, a boy from Group thirteen. He is fading slowly away into the bed. He wants sweets which we give him and he puts under his pillow for later. Teresa meets little blind boy Sergei who has been to Ireland previously. She passes on Biddy's love to him.

Unit Five is improved. The improvements in Group Four are because of our visits. We have to change attitudes. Including our own. But how? Wouldn't you think by now at least there would be something rubbing off? Or are we just tired out after all the travel and inclined to see the problems rather than the improvements. Meanwhile, our men are working away putting in showers and baths to try to improve the hygiene end of things. They have done enormous work in the week. It is just amazing. But where is the good of it if the children are hungry? What was the point in sending tonnes of clothes if the children need food? If we buy food, will they give it to them? That is the ultimate question!

We leave the orphanage. Worn out. Disconsolate. There is no answer here in this place.

Later we send several tonnes of clothes to the jail in Gomel. Mostly thermal caps for everyone and thousands of pairs of underwear for all the women. We are informed that some of the stuff was stolen. What do you expect? We sent the stuff to a jail. Some of the thermal hats were seen on people in down town

Gomel. We thought about doing another trip back to gather up our hats. We also considered the possibility of seeking out the underwear down town in Gomel. Excuse me, missus, by any chance are you wearing …? We cancelled the trip.

At the airport as time for departure approached there was more trauma. Firstly, Ned had no ticket. In Shannon as he had departed, the steward had obviously taken both outward and return parts of the ticket and nobody noticed until now. Several severe-looking people in various uniforms surrounded our Ned as though he were a major terrorist instead of a mere Christian Brother and he was escorted aside for questioning. Next the men with their tools and workgear were being weighed in and found to have several kilos over weight. But they refused to pay up any extra money for extra weight, seeing that they had been on voluntary work helping out this blessed country. Loud voices began to emerge from the check-in desk.

The group of children travelling back with us arrived from Cherven Orphanage. There were no tickets for them. The group of children travelling back with us from Goradishche failed to arrive and we were approaching check-in closure time. There were also no tickets for this group.

I kept saying all will be well, it will all work out as I kept one eye on Teresa, with Sergei in her arms, making her way gently and quietly through ticket inspection, through baggage control, all the way as far as Passport control. Here, I could see there was a general pause as several documents were checked and advice sought from higher authorities. Would they refuse to allow Sergei return home with us? I could see Teresa holding Sergei calmly yet knew how heavy he was. How long would she have to stand there? There are times when little quiet prayers to little loving angels become very significant. Gently, the logjam broke and Teresa and Sergei headed for the departure gate. Relief, at last. Ned was sorted out, the men were let through, the children arrived, the tickets were found. Relief all round. As often happens in this country, everything gets solved in the end. The greatest relief was seeing Teresa and Sergei heading for that departure gate.

Following them went each of the men and women workers

after their hard week's work, each bearing a handicapped child with them on the journey home. I watched them on the plane as they held on to their child, each child asleep in the arms of a weary, exhausted man; each seatful a madonna-embrace of the goodness of people with love in their hearts. Good people. Weary, worn out. But, oh so good! I made my way up to where Teresa was sitting with Sergei as there was still filming to be done. We were still in our same clothes for continuity in the televsion programme. As we banked left over Poland heading for home, Teresa whispered to me:

'Liam, don't tell Margaret (our producer) but I've a different perfume on today'.

CHAPTER TEN

Heal thyself

Throughout these journeys into lives and into places we could have never imagined, we have travelled with our friends and neighbours. All of them are extraordinary people in their own way. Some of them are extra special in that their story seems to reflect a new meaning, beyond the usual. There is a deeper connection, an almost surreal link, a different aspect. An aspect which brings humour and sense to the story. An aspect which digs deep in to the heart and uproots the filaments of emotion hidden within us. It is this aspect of his story which makes Paddy's place in it special.

Paddy is himself an orphan. He has memories that we do not have. His story is different and it is beautiful. It makes connections in a real way, in a way that we might miss as we did not travel the same path. Paddy's story is a special story and though the story may not be finished it has many beautiful chapters. This story is intertwined with our story and the story of the orphans of Belarus orphanages. It has been a special thing to travel this story with Paddy and to connect with some of the feelings of this man. It has been an emotional and absolute pleasure. It has been just so unexpected, so special and so much fun. We have shared many happy moments and we have felt the throb of sadness and of loneliness in his heart as he seeks out his brother and sister from his real, his birth family. It has been beautiful to be part of that journey and that search with Paddy.

His eyes were opened. He could see again

How're things?

Fine. How're your things?

Oh, my things are fine! Never better! Come on in and meet Mom.

Mom, this is Liam.

Hello Mom.

Hello Liam. You're the Christian Brother. Paddy is always talking about you. I had two you know. Paddy and another boy, Francis. The other boy died in England. I adopted the two of them. Two great boys. I've a bad leg. I was going down to the doctor the other day with it and then I didn't go at all. I said sure what would the doctor know, 'tis my leg. Wasn't I right. It's paining though. Here, look at it.

What age are you?

I'm eighty-four.

Didn't it last a long time?

Feck you. What? Two great boys! Francis died in England. That's a picture of him there on the wall. Paddy went over, he knew there was something wrong. He went over and found him. He was only thirty four. I took them in years ago. I needn't tell you we hadn't much. I was afraid of my life I would lose them again. A girl used come out from the orphanage to see that everything was Ok, and they hid inside in the wardrobe. Afraid of their life they were that they'd have to go back. I couldn't have children so I got them. Great lads. Paddy, make a drop of punch there for Brian.

His name is Liam.

Sorry Liam. I get mixed up. But sure Brian doesn't mind. Sure you don't, Brian? Brian, I'm going to tell you now them were tough times. We had nothing. And my husband died after adopting the two boys. I didn't know what to do. But I said I'd keep them. I'll tell you, now, I often went to bed hungry so that they'd have something. Not a word of a lie. And many more like me. We hadn't much then. They were different times. It was a different world. But sure I couldn't let them back. Paddy was small, only four. I don't know why I picked him. Maybe because he was so small.

I was so cute.

That's true, you were. Will you go in and make a drop of punch? Lilly, where's Lilly? She's very good. It's not easy with two women in the house. The children are very good. Laura is mad about the football. The boys are very good. Sometimes though I get mad with them. But what can you say. They're very good. David is very thoughtful. Always looking after Nana. Thomas is a great boy. And Justin is very good. They're all very good in fairness. Thank God.

Do you remember the orphanage, Paddy?

I remember it all right. The rows of beds and waiting for the food. I don't remember being hungry, just lining up waiting. A short while after coming here I saw two nuns in Lahinch and ran after them calling 'Mama , Mama'. I thought 'twas my mother. That's all I knew. I didn't know any better. I have a mother somewhere, maybe brothers and sisters. One brother anyway, maybe one sister. I'm trying to find them. It's not easy. Sure they could be in America or anywhere. But I'll find them. You must give me a hand.

Sure , whatever I can do ! Anyway, Paddy, I must be off.

Ok, Liam. 'Twas lovely having you.

Bye, Paddy. 'Twas lovely being had!

Later, Paddy came with us to Belarus, on one of our first trips. The trip included visits to orphanages and some long train journeys. In Yastrebel orphanage there was a problem with mice but Paddy solved this by taking a picture of a cat from a box of chocolates and putting the picture standing near the mousehole so that the mouse would be frightened and the girls wouldn't. We had great fun on that trip. We travelled by train to the various locations and spent the time telling yarns and jokes and drinking 'choot-choots ', shots of the local vodka.

As we travelled on, we passed Luninets, the place where I had been teaching. We were not stopping this time but I was able to show them the hospital building. 'That, lads, is where we showed the Russians how to drink. It was about eight o'clock in the morning. John Morgan was with me. They call him Petrovich because his father was Peter. He is from Kilfenora, Céilí Band and set-dancing country. Anyway, we presented the Director of the hospital with the thousands of pounds worth of medicines and of course there had to be a drink. Remember now it was eight o'clock in the morning. The vodka and slices of orange were brought out. We had a couple of 'chootchoots', the small Russian glasses which are filled with vodka neat and you are expected to throw them back straight. John decided to take these guys on at this hour of the morning. There was a large crystal vase on the table with four roses. John grabbed the vase, took the roses out, threw the water on the floor and said: 'Here! Would ye ever give us a decent drink and stop the feck-acting round with those small drops.' Kilfenora 1, Luninets 0. Up the Banner!

Later Paddy had the help of a not-very-good interpreter as we attended a function with the director and heads of a good orphanage.
'Is that a collective farm?'
'Sorry, Paddy I do not understand you '.
'Would they have many cows on that farm?'
'Sorry, Paddy I do not understand you '.
'Does the state pay the workers on the farm?'
'Sorry, Paddy I do not understand you '.
'How much money would they get working there, the workers?'
'Sorry, Paddy I do not understand you.'
'Feck you , if I asked you for a kiss you'd know what I was saying '.
'Sorry, Paddy I do not understand you.'

Later, as we got ready to launch the first ever St Patrick's Day Parade in Minsk, we discussed life and work and Paddy explained that as well as working as driver at Cullinan's Builders Providers, he is also trained as an embalmer for the undertaking service.
'I could do a lovely job on you. Embalming, make-up, the works. Make you look real nice .'
'Maybe you could do it for me now. Look at the state of me. And they'll all be there at the parade full of style. Lads, we're really letting the side down.'
'Sure, we're not too bad,' said Breada, 'Won't we do?'
'Really though, I could fix up everything to look well. In fairness lads, some of them don't know what they're doing. I was at a

funeral in Limerick last week and the poor lady looked so terrible, no bit of proper care taken at all. But I've all those courses done '.

'Some of the jobs must be terrible, Paddy.'

'Indeed they are. Dreadful! You have no idea! If someone is very bad before they die, sure they nearly fall apart. Or if there is a bad accident, God forbid or someone is run over. It can be terrible. But I can do all the jobs. Even Francis, my brother who died over in England. I laid him out.'

'It's not easy, Paddy.'

'It's not, but anyone in that job must have respect for the person who has died. If you don't then you shouldn't be in it. You have to respect the dead.'

'Do you sleep afterwards, or would it bother you, Paddy?'

'Not a bother. Sure they're only people even if they're dead and I am happy when I've done a good job. I'll do a good job on you too when you're gone, God forbid.'

'Take care, fear you leave one hand on me. Liam, that fecker isn't to touch me. I'll be cremated first '.

And so the banter went on as we threshed our way along on the powerful old locomotives of the Belarus railways, sometimes singing and laughing, leaving on a jet plane, not knowing when I'll be back again, wheeling a wheelbarrow through streets broad and narrow, deep inside a forest where there's a door into another world, it being on the twenty third of June the day before the fair and lonely round the fields of Athenry. Sometimes in the middle of the mix up of songs in our heads we sat in simple quiet as we thought of the children ahead or pondered on the places we had been. In and out through the fun and crack, there was always the sense that we were dealing with children, with orphans and sometimes with a side of ourselves that might prove tender. Paddy was one of us, our brother, who had himself been in an orphanage and been one of the lucky ones in having been chosen by Mom to come and live in Liscannor. Now, we headed back into the orphanages and into places in Paddy's heart where the tender and sore spots might still exist. As indeed they did exist! And so when we came to Kobrin home for small children we came face to face with Paddy's past and with our love for this big man with a big, soft auld heart that embraced and joked with us all. Sheer goodness.

There were many children in the room and we went to share sweets with them, to see how and where they lived and just to look. We each picked up a child and I saw Paddy picking himself up in an orphanage many miles and years away, another time in another place but the same situation. We each stood with a child in embrace and listened quietly to our sobs and watched each others' tears as we embraced these children and embraced our Paddy in his past and in whatever he felt from then and now.

Later Paddy told us:

'We always waited to be picked up. When someone would come to the orphanage, we waited and hoped we would be picked up. Some times we were picked up. I was always put down again. Until Mom came … '

And on we trundled again through the October of Belarus, trying to feel what it was like and knowing as we saw winter arriving around us, somehow there would be a spring, better days. And I wondered about Paddy's family, his real brother and sister. Could we ever even know where to begin to find them? Would it be possible? Who knows? God is good! And on we went, each person looking out a different window and each looking into our souls, hearing Sonia O'Brien playing the Coolin in the Boghill recesses of our minds, bearing our tears and emotions through time and space into healed and unhealed crevices as the light from our souls leaked through.

CHAPTER ELEVEN

It was early in the morning and still dark

The title of the book was going to be the numbers 'forty-six, thirty-one, thirty-six', referring to the ages of three people. Three children from one family separated when they were young and sent off to orphanages here in Ireland in the days when life was different and perhaps not as tolerant as it is now. The three people were Paddy and his brother Michael and sister Helen. It is so moving to be working with orphan children and, at the same time, to be working with someone who is an orphan himself and is in the process of trying to find his family. Paddy was like that, looking and searching and hoping that he would find his family, hoping that they were out there somewhere. Paddy had an adoptive brother, Francis, who unfortunately died unexpectedly at a very young age. This was a very low point in life, to have had a brother and then suddenly he is gone. Yet it was from under that blanket of darkness that Paddy found his real brother, Michael, and together they managed to find their sister.

I was very privileged to be involved in a small way in that story, a story which Paddy will one day tell himself. For now, it is also part of the story of the children we are meeting and Paddy's story represents the hope we have for these children. We hope that they too will find out who they are, that they will find their brothers and sisters. We hope that they will recover from the situation where they were not wanted by their parents or had parents in such a position of being unable to look after them. We pray that, somehow, by the grace of the good God, they will find the little bit of love in life which makes life worth living. It is one of the reasons why each death of a child in one of the orphanages is the seed of pain for those who may be seeking that child in the future. Paddy has found his brother and sister. All three are together again. As it should be.

'Everyone is looking for you'

On Monday morning the phone rang. It was Helen. I could not believe it. This was the voice that Paddy and Michael had been waiting to hear for thirty-one years. On the previous week I had contacted the parish priest of her parish to ask if he knew her family and if he would be kind enough to call and make discreet enquiry about whether Helen wished to be contacted by her long lost brothers. Only days before, Helen had been talking with her husband, Terry, and family about the possibility of searching for any brothers or sisters out there. On Sunday night, following the visit of their priest, her parents called out to her house and broke the news to her – she had two brothers and they would like to meet. The meeting would take place only if she wanted and if her family agreed. That was Sunday night.

I had decided I would ring back Fr Stokes on Monday evening to see if he had had any luck contacting the family. But that morning the phone rang in school.

'Hello. This is Helena.'

Contact! I could have jumped through the roof to realise what those four words meant, what it would mean to Paddy and Michael. Here I was with this treasure which they had sought for the past twenty years. It was Michael who began the search when he found that he had a brother and sister. He went to enormous trouble to find more information, to follow any possible clue as to where the members of his beloved family were. It wasn't easy for Michael. His had been the hard life. He had slaved for a pittance over the years as he was fostered out to various works. He is a kind, gentle soul who only wanted to bring together the three who had been scattered over the past forty six years. Only he knows the thoughts and worries and fears about where his brother and sister were. All those years he looked forward to contact, just to know that their life had been better, that they were well. It would be a dream to actually meet up and hold in his arms the boy and girl he knew were out there. Only for Ownie Ward and a few others Michael might not have even made it. They were the loyal supporters who encouraged him along the way and kept hold of his story.

The search was not an easy one. Not being great with the biro, as he says himself, Michael did all in his power to follow any lead he could. In his own way, he brought his own bits of identification together. A copy of his provisional driving licence, a letter from the dole office … his identification in the world in the hope that it would be helpful.

In the meantime Paddy was in Liscannor with his happy family and wondering what he could do on a similar quest. By miracle, coincidence and good fortune Paddy and Michael made contact three years ago and enjoyed their first Christmas together as an almost complete family in 1996. Then the search began in earnest for the sister they knew was out there. First word from official sources said she was in America. The search seemed too much. Where would she be? What would her name be? How in the name of God would one go about trying to find a person with a new name in America?

Further searching and further following of small clues brought the search to Ireland again. Only Paddy and Michael know the twists and turns, the legal, legitimate means and the human contacts that brought about the situation where they ended up with an address. We were in the middle of the Cherven Chernobyl orphans visit when Paddy one day said, 'I know where my sister is.' After all these years, 'I know where my sister is.' The question then was how to approach her and her family. Their concern was always that she be gently and sensitively approached. And even though both men would have jumped into the car and raced to her door, they held back. How was she? How would she react? Did she know anything about it? Had she had a good life? Was she married? Did her husband know her story? Would she want to meet them? All the questions raced and raged and patiently they tried to think of a sensitive way to make gentle contact.

This is where I did my small bit, I made a phone call. The parish priest of her parish said he would find a way to sensitively make known the request to make contact. If the family did not wish to meet, there would be no pressure. Imagine wanting to meet someone all your life, carrying your love and your fears for them everyday and then when you know where they are saying we will meet only if you want it. We respect your views so much that we will carry our dreams and fears forever rather than intrude and upset you. We have loved you always and will continue to do so quietly, in the unknown, if you wish. These are beautiful men! And so it was beautiful too when the phone rang on Monday 30 November and a voice said:

'Hello. This is Helena.'

Together with Paddy and his family, we left at half seven on Saturday morning and drove to Galway to pick up Michael. He was all excited and spruced up. This was it, this was the day. The week had been long, waiting ... the night had been long, afraid of not waking up, afraid that he might die in his sleep on the night before meeting his sister and might miss the chance of a lifetime. The journey to the hotel passed eventually and we arrived at 1.20 outside the Glen Royal.

Would she be here? She had seen the photos that I sent on, would she recognise the lads. In we went and there inside was this beautiful young lady and her man.

'Are you Brother Liam?'

'Yes, are you Helen? This is your brother Michael ... and your brother Paddy ... and his wife, Lilly.'

'This is my husband Terry.'

And there it was. Tears and fears, joys and nerves. They hugged and Paddy went off to the toilet for a cry. It was wonderful. She looks like them and thinks like them and is the spitting image of Paddy's Thomas. And when she was young she looked like Paddy with long hair. And Michael tells all the story, of his search and his life, and Paddy tells about his family and Mom, and Helen tells her part with Terry joining in and everyone all emotional, wanting to talk and not wanting to talk, wanting to just sit and enjoy the miracle of the whole day. And I sat and watched as they related their stories and tried to make sense of what they had been through. And I watched Helen sitting between the two boys and thought how easily it would have been for this not to happen, how easily they might never have made the contact. And how awful it would have been to have this beautiful girl out there and these two men searching for her in America or even in Ireland and it never to happen.

'Youse are great to come all the way,' said Helen.

'We would have gone to America ... we would have gone to Africa for you if we thought you were there.'

And they sat and spoke about their mother and why she had

given them up for adoption and the pain she must have felt and the society that existed then which made giving up babies a better option. And they must live with that whole question of looking back and wondering why, even as they rejoice in their meeting and continue to live and love their own families. The boys gave Helen a card 'For a Special Sister ' and I couldn't help thinking that this is the first time in forty-six years that Michael has had a sister and he remembers to pick a card and bring it with him for her, and Paddy and Michael both sign it to mark their meeting with this special sister.

Their story is their story to tell in their own time. It was wonderful to be there, wonderful and tearful and emotional and wonderful. Mobile phones made it possible for each to report home and say that they were all wonderful and for Michael to speak to Helen's mother and Helen to speak to Paddy's Mom and half of the county it seemed. And Paddy told Helen's Mom what a 'wonderful job you have made of your daughter' and everyone rejoiced as the little contacts were made between the different worlds.

Time to go, to say thanks and say bye for now. Time to stand under the Christmas Tree and have a few photographs of the two boys and their sister. Another photo with Paddy's wife, Lilly, and Helen's husband, Terry. Then time to say goodbye. That final hug. And in that hug there is no end, as Michael holds on to Helen and then Michael and Helen and Paddy, they hold on to each other and know that now, now, there will be no letting go.

And we looked on and cried, knowing what it all meant.

Helen and Paddy and Michael don't know one another for long, but they know they belong together. And Helen must know by now that had she come to that meeting with nothing, in rags, these two wonderful men who have sought her so long would have seen nothing but their special sister whom they have always and will always love. Wonderful!

'I never expected to meet anyone like her, not in my dreams,' said Michael.

And we remember being in the orphanage, picking up the children and putting them down again and being left there. And we feel the pain of those children who are always put down again. And we wonder, if it is possible for a family to meet up again like this, then maybe it is possible to carry on this battle, to make a life for these other forgotten ones so that they too may have a life and find in the future someone who loves them, and even someone who is their brother or sister, someone who is even now holding them in his dreams and looking forward to the day of meeting up again. Maybe it is possible. Time now just to sit and enjoy the miracle. Time to remember the hug under the Christmas Tree which squeezed to life the bond of family, which embraced the hunger for the lost one and wrapped it in a strength of kindness and love which no amount of separation could overcome.

'We would have come to America, to Africa if we thought you were there.'

And they would have, on their knees, if necessary. And let that not go unsaid, that such haunted and haunting love still exists in this world, in the hearts and minds of men for whom life maybe wasn't a bed of roses but who still held on to goodness and decency and love, and the hope of meeting a sister they felt they had, keeping a grasp on the essentials, the important things. Always.

CHAPTER TWELVE

Sasha

When I was about sixteen, I met my mother for the first time. Maybe I knew her when I was very small but my mind holds no memories of that time. When you are sixteen, after spending your life in various orphanages, maybe it is better not to have memories. Memories of what? Of a happy home? Childhood? Care and attention? Memories of smiles and of being wanted? No such memories in my mind. When I met my mother, I met a woman. A woman who cried when she saw me but a woman for whom I have no tears. She is the woman who gave birth to me but there is no love bond. What love? What bond? She drinks. Like many of the people in this land. In my family. In my life. In the lives of so many like me who have emerged into life from the cover-up world that is the orphanages for those diagnosed as oligophrenic, idiot or imbecile. There is no other diagnosis for the unwanted because there is no other place to go. There are no other options. To create another diagnosis would mean a responsibility to provide another level of care. It is easier to class us all together. Then we don't need care. I went home with this woman when I was sixteen, to spend some time with her. It is a place she calls home but it is not home to me. My home is in my head, safe from the walls of confining orphanages and safe from the people who lay claim to part of me. My home is in my head but in my head there is no place called home.

When I was so young I cannot remember I was taken from this woman my mother or sent by her to another woman, her mother. My grandmother looked after me then, as home was not home to me even then. I have some memories of this woman, my grandmother. I cried when she died last year. Her life and my links with her life were buried together. In a grave. Six foot by two. When my grandmother could no longer cope with me or when she had to work to survive, I was sent to a school, a board-

ing school, an *internat*. At the age of four or younger, I do not remember. Like so many more hundreds of children in our country, we are institutionalised. For many it is better than home. For
none, it is home. There is food. There is a bed and a roof. And the
knowledge that tomorrow will be the same as today. Safe. A repeat of today. But safe. Here, at the age of five, Dima doesn't
have to beat his father with a stool when he comes home drunk
again and begins to beat his mother. Here that doesn't happen.
Maybe there is little love here but there is also little hate. There is
little emotion. Little expressed. Here, little Artur, aged three,
doesn't have to peel his own potatoes and try to cook them like
he would have to at home. He gets more than the bread and
water or milk he would sometimes get at home. Here can sometimes be better than home. But it is never home.

When I was sent to this new place I was excited. Once I had
made some friends, it was good. I remember the layout of the
rooms. Where the boys were. Where the girls were. I remember
the small tables and chairs. Where we ate. The washing areas
and the hallway. My brother and sister were in this place also
but we had little contact and so the bonds of family began to
stretch into far flung places. It did not matter then. It doesn't
matter much now either. But there are people who are my brothers and sisters. In name at least. I was friends with a boy called
Dima, then. But I don't know where he is now or what happened to him. He was part of my life for a while, part of this
place. Then. Sometime.

Later, at some stage, I was moved to another house for the
three degrees of invalid disability – oligophrenia, idiot and imbecile. My first days were spend in isolation. In case of contamination. Am I infectious? Is it a disease to be unwanted? To have
no-one able to care for me? When I am small? I waited looking
through the grille on the window wanting to be with the other
children, wanting to be part of something, even if it wasn't
home. But it could be home to me – for a while.

I was put in group nine with children who were not so clever
but not so stupid. Sasha was my new best friend then. The food
in this place was much worse and much less than in the former
place. We were always hungry and we had work to do.

At one stage a commission of special people came to examine

us, to see if there were some of us clever enough to go to a hand-icapped school where there was education and training. I wanted to get out of this place. I wanted to go. I wanted to learn. But up to now I had never had proper lessons. I couldn't read or write. I wanted to go. Luckily, I was chosen as brainy and with some others we left and headed for my third boarding-school.

I remember the first day, the room I was shown into that would be mine for the next while. Later, I met the others. A new place is always strange until you make new friends. Then there are links and contacts, smiles and sharing. It is not so bad then. I was inquisitive. I wanted to see everything, where everything was, how everything worked. I made many new friends. Another Dima became my best friend here. His legs didn't work properly. One was shorter than the other and he wobbled along. I saw him once maybe a year ago. Maybe longer.

In class my desk-mate was Marina. She is my first love. Marina couldn't walk. She was in a wheelchair. She was the best pupil in the class. We sat beside one another then. Part of me wanted to kiss her sometimes but I didn't know how. How to kiss, how to make contact, how to reach out.

Some of the people here, the children, some of them had par-ents. A few came to visit sometimes. They brought presents, sweets. No-one brought me sweets. No-one came to see me. Yet, somewhere at some stage in my memory, my granny, the mother of the woman who is my mother who cried when she saw me, came to visit. It is long ago. A faded possible-memory. Or a memory I have created because some part of me wants it to be so.

Anna Petrovna loved me. She was a great teacher then. She helped me all the time. I had never had proper classes so I couldn't read or write like the others. Anna Petrovna gave me special time after class to help me to read. I didn't make much progress but being with Anna Petrovna after class wasn't just about lessons. It was being with someone who cared enough to spend that time with me. I still keep contact with her. I wasn't a good pupil. I didn't want to work. I couldn't do the lessons. I didn't want to do them then. But I was great at physical exercises class. I didn't smoke or drink then and always got five out of five in this class. I could run very fast. I was a very fast runner. This was a happy time. It was a good place. The big boys and the big girls loved me there too. I know I was loved. I was a nice boy, a good boy. They loved me. But it came to an end and I was sent away again. And Anna Petrovna cried after me. I remember that. I remember Anna Petrovna crying when I had to leave.

It was because of another boy called Dima. He was a big boy but had come with me from the last boarding-house. He was a good worker, especially in the summer when we worked in the fields doing the hay and the potatoes. Dima worked hard there also. One day, there was some writing done on a board in a room. Somehow the board was set on fire and burnt. It was a big problem then. I was blamed with Dima for it. We had come from the same place. We would be sent back together. One brush. All tarred. So back we went, after being threatened with the police. Back we went. Anna Petrovna's tears trickled down behind us, in my mind. Later, she phoned many times to see if I was Ok. She warned me not to do any bad things. She tried to get me back. But there was no going back. Only back to where I had come from.

On the journey back to group nine, I cried. I cried for the bad food ahead and the love for me that I left behind. I cried for Anna Petrovna, looking out the back window of the car. Later, I forgot everything. It can be better to forget. Let it go into the past wherever that is. Yet life goes on. At least the Director of this place then was a good man. And the deputy Director then was better. We had a good relationship. That helps. When ten of your thirteen years have been spent in institutions, it is good to have a decent relationship with the people in charge.

For us, it was a big treat to smoke. We didn't know how to smoke. Someone gave one of the boys some cigarettes one day and we began to practice. We coughed many times. At some stage when we were in hospital for a check-up, we were warned not to smoke. There is a check-up for everyone when they are teenagers. I was told that if I smoked it would cause a big lump in my head. I have smoked for many years now. I am still alive. Where is the big lump? Why haven't I died? Smoking is bad. We smoked anyway. It was something to do.

The deputy Director helped me one day. We were good friends. We had spent a terrible long day working in the fields.

We were ravenous. When we got back to the orphanage we were all starving. All healthy young men at work all day in the fields. When we went to the kitchen, our food was served. A small bit on each plate. Three spoons and it was gone. I looked in the saucepans which the kitchen workers were carrying round and there was loads of food – potatoes and *casha* porridge and pieces of chicken. I grabbed one of the women by the hair and pushed her across the tables. She went tumbling across the tables. Then I emptied the saucepans onto the table and said: 'Here, children, eat!' We all grabbed and ate with our hands. We just grabbed the food and stuffed it into our mouths we were that hungry. I was mad. It wasn't fair. We had worked hard, the food was there, we were hungry and entitled to it. When I am mad, I am very strong. They sent for one of the bigger boys to control me. To pin my arms behind my back. They sent for the old doctor with his sedative injection. I managed to break free in the commotion and the injection ended up in the doctor's behind. Not in me. He began to get drowsy and had to waddle off to sleep.

The deputy Director came and I was called aside. We sat and talked. I told him the story. How we worked. How hungry we were. I showed him the saucepans of food. He agreed with me. There was no more trouble for me. No injections. The other boys didn't react when they were hungry. They haven't as strong a character as I have. I am sorry for the woman whom I pushed. It was just that we were so hungry. After that, I wouldn't work in the fields. Later too, there was a new deputy Director.

Later, I was put in group ten. Here, we worked on the farm. Cheap labour picking apples and potatoes. Everyone did it. I had friends then, Vova and Valera. They are still there. I hated being confined. I wanted to get out, to get free. To go walking like we used to in the last place. No-one came to visit either. Not here. No visits of the children. No-one brought presents. No-one brought me sweets.

Then one day we heard some people were coming to visit, some Irish people, some foreigners. Vita and I were chosen to help with the visitors. Two new coats were brought out for us so that we would look well when the visitors came. We didn't know what to expect but we were told that if we were good there would be sweets. There were! Sweets for everyone. We carried the boxes around to each of the thirteen groups and helped give out the sweets. We got fistfulls. Fistfulls of sweets. Someone came with sweets.

I remember Anne going out for a cigarette. I didn't know her name then but she pointed to herself and said: 'Anne'. Then she pointed at me: 'Sasha'. We watched as she lit a cigarette. She knew what we wanted. 'Here, sure if they want them in this place, give it to them. Can't they have a cigarette?' It was five years ago. I was fourteen. Fourteen when I got sweets and a cigarette.

Before they left, I got a present of a book. They put some money in it. Dollars. More money than we had ever had. More than we had ever seen. We had never had money. Even though we worked. That evening we had a big feed. We bought sweets and biscuits and salami for everyone. We share them out in the group. Twenty dollars bought a lot then. We had some extra for many evenings. The Director was amazed at all the stuff we had. Food for several days. It was great. After that I tried to do everything as best I could for the Director so that he would choose me again to help when the Irish people came back. If they came back. We hoped they would come again. It gave us hope when there was no hope. There was hope for more sweets and good times. For once, something to look forward to.

I remember the day we were called to group four. We were to help bringing a child out who was lying asleep. We picked him up and brought him out. All the time he was asleep. I remember thinking – why is he asleep? Why doesn't he wake up? All the time he was asleep. Even when we put him in the old ambulance he was asleep. We took him to the hospital. Then we brought him into a room where other people, old and young, some children, were asleep. There were twins there asleep, very alike. We put the boy in this room. It was cold there. He was only skin and bone. Like a skeleton. But he was asleep. Later, I understood about autopsy examinations and knew why this boy stayed asleep. Children died regularly in group four and we brought them out. We didn't think of them as people. It was like bones for a dog. We didn't like going there. Now, the Irish have come and they feed the children. Now there are children there. People. Before, there were not children, not individuals. Only sometimes people who went to sleep and we took them to the morgue at the hospital. You don't understand what it was like. You can't understand. Because now it is different.

When we heard the Irish people were coming back, there was great excitement. We thought there will be more sweets and food again. We made sure to be good so that we would be around to help when they came. When they did arrive, they had sweets and presents. And they hugged us. There wasn't much of that here. It was a world of individuals. Not hugs. Soon we heard that some children were invited to Ireland. It would be by aeroplane. I didn't know where Ireland was, only that it was far away. I hoped I would be one of the ones to go. I was. Maybe because I had helped. Maybe because Liam remembered my name. Maybe I was lucky.

On the aeroplane, I cried all the way. People around were all looking at me. I just sat there and cried. It was all new. Frightening, I suppose. All my life I had lived in an internat, an orphanage, an institution. And now for the first time, I was leaving that place. A place with a routine and a certain safety. Predictable. Nothing ever changed so it was always a place to be sure of. Not that it was bad, but it just wasn't home. It wasn't what children growing up need. But now as I left it, I cried. I didn't know what would happen. Where I was going. I was afraid. So I cried.

When the plane landed in Shannon, Liam met us on the runway. At least a face we knew. I felt unsure but I was welcomed. Everything was new. I helped with the luggage and then we went off in a minibus. To Ennistymon, to a big house. I wanted to see everything again. To check everything out. It was strange not speaking the same language as these Irish friends. Then I met Anne who had given me the cigarettes. Over the weeks I made good friends and would like to stay there. But the first night, I cried all the time. I didn't want to be there. I wanted to be back in the confines of my breaking world, the only world I knew. Now, for me, Ireland is the best place. My dream.

It had to end and we came back. Later, after that I got the chance to go to a training school, a vocational school. I still couldn't read or write so it was difficult but I didn't need much to learn some basic plumbing. I also know how to repair tape-recorders. I like to do this. When two years were up I was given some work in a small town, the birthplace of my parents. The place where I was registered. Where I am to live and work. There was little work there. The other men, many of them were drinkers, let me do the heavy work. For my month's work, I got about seven thousand roubles, about five dollars for the month. I couldn't even have bread every day. Bread and milk sometimes. Yet, this is where I must work. This is where I must live. The state gives you a place to live if you are from an institution. Some place to live in the town where you are registered. I am entitled to a flat but someone else lives in it. No-one did the proper documents while I was in the orphanages so now it is gone. I am a product of an institution. So instead the state gave me a room, an empty room attached to the back of an ancient post-office in the town. No toilet. No water. No cooker. Nothing at all. I had to provide from my earnings. How to live in our country?

I did not want to live in this place. I could not live in this place. It is a nice town but I know no-one there. I want to go back to Cherven, where I know people. Where people know me. But where to live? Only with the help of the Irish people can I hope to have a home.

Later I got another chance to go to Ireland for a holiday. I helped with some jobs. Some people gave me money, I can do good work. When I came back I bought a motorbike. I always wanted a bike. I know how to take it apart and clean it and put it back together again. I work on it everyday in the summer. In winter you cannot use a motorbike here. Because of the weather. But now I have a bike. It is the best bike here. But I don't have a licence. Because I was in the internat, because I have been diagnosed as invalid. I am not stupid. I can do work. I can repair bikes. But I cannot get a licence for a motorbike because I was in the orphanage. Because of other people's problems. It is like that here. You get locked into the system. It can be impossible to get out again. To become a person again.

But I have friends. And I have my bike. Thanks to people in Ireland. In Lahinch.

CHAPTER THIRTEEN

A farmer went out to plant the seed

How many children there are like Paddy in Belarus orphanages is difficult to quantify. How many are there like Sasha is just a statistic. How many children there have a family, how many have a brother or sister in another orphanage is difficult to find out. Some may have a sibling in the very same orphanage as themselves and be unaware or have very little contact. How many of them will ever have a chance of a life outside the orphanage is also easy to compute. Very few. So, all we know is that we must try to help them all. Not just the few lucky enough or sick enough to get to come to Ireland but all of them no matter where they are. We especially want to help all the handicapped children, all those who feel unloved or unwanted.

Paddy is one of our people and life has brought him back together with his family. Sergei is one child of grace who has found a loving home and brought much love to many people. But there are so many similar children. The problem for us was how could we help them all, how could we make a real difference in their lives and in the conditions in which they lived. We had to try to change the entire place. This meant beginning with the very basics. We needed to get enough clothes, shoes, soap, shampoo and all the ordinary things that children need to live some sort of half decent life. So operation Donkey Trail, the Humanitarian Aid delivery programme, began in earnest. But where to begin? And how?

Having the right person in the right place at the right time is a huge advantage for any group. So it turned out when we began to try to solve this transporting-of-goods problem. Not having a clue where to begin it was Helen, who worked in Elite Kamino International Freight Company in Shannon, who got the whole thing underway. Firstly, this meant doing documents for customs on this side of the world. Then we needed to locate a clearing company in Minsk to arrange completion of documents and delivery of cargo from Minsk airport to the orphanage.

'We'll try it with a few boxes,' said Helen and so the cargo side of the business began.

It was great fun considering we didn't speak Russian at the time and in Minsk they didn't speak English. This first shipment from Shannon was duly boxed, labelled and all documents prepared. Belavia Airlines were very happy to have cargo to ferry to Minsk and so off went the first shipment. Several weeks later they still hadn't been delivered as the Minsk side of operations didn't come through. The company we had contacted just didn't bother or perhaps didn't know how to do the paperwork or perhaps were unable for the mental leap required to engage in business with an overseas partner. Anyway it didn't work. Enter Boris, stage left, complete with Eastern Health Board Ambulance and operation delivery got underway. Boris was part of Maria's group in Minsk and well used to dealing with officialdom and documents. For him, it was also a new learning experience but he managed to find his way around customs in Minsk and sort out a system that worked. He then delivered the goods to the orphanages as we instructed. Millions of panadol, boxes of toothbrushes, acres of clothes were shipped – to Pinsk to share with poor families; to Cherven for all the two hundred and fifty children; to Goradishche for the two hundred children; to Minsk to the Association of Mothers who keep their handicapped child at home; to Gomel jail for the women in prison; to Kobrin for those in the children's village.

Week by week the shipments went. Hank arrived each week to fill his vanload from the monastery. We had the packing done, the boxes labelled and the lists ready. Helen cleared documents with customs and Hank delivered to the cargo bay in Shannon airport and away it went. Regular as clockwork.

Stuff began to arrive from all over the place. Several huge containers of female hygiene products arrived from Dublin. The boys from the school were helping us load them on to Patsy's truck for deliver to Shannon. 'What's in the boxes? They're very heavy,' said one boy. 'Books,' said Helen. And that kept them happy.

Later as the shipment became larger and the goods heavier

we had to begin shipping by road. This meant getting forty-foot lorries loaded and ready for transportation across Europe to Belarus. More paperwork. More documents. But also more aid and at a cheaper rate than air-freight costs. Filling lorries then became regular business. Of course sorting and packing boxes was a huge time-consuming job. Each evening we met in the hall and began sorting out the good from the bad, then into piles of children's, adult female and male before packing it all into boxes. It was long, tedious work and hard to keep track of everything. One evening Phil came to help and made the mistake of taking off her coat and leaving it down with her handbag. I packed her coat and was in the process of packing her handbag when I noticed there was something in it. 'Hey lads, here's a bag with something in it. Whoever gave it must have forgotten to search it!' 'Well, look at him off with my one and only handbag and the last few bob I've left and he going to send it to Belarus. Give me back my bag, you eejit!' Just in time as we would have had to open all the boxes and go through them all again to find Phil's handbag.

The island of Inis Oirr is the smallest of the beautiful Aran Island lying just west of Doolin in North Clare. Doolin is famous as the centre of Irish music, traditional and as it should be. From Doolin pier you can stand and look out to see the white lighthouse of Inis Oirr across the sometimes turbulent waters. Out there, Josephine did a mighty collection of clothes from all the islanders and arranged shipment back to us. We then would load up and send it all to Belarus. 'I had terrible trouble finding boxes for it all,' said Josephine. 'I phoned a computer firm to ask for boxes but they said they couldn't give us any as all the boxes had the logo on the side. So, then I phoned the cardboard box factory. They sent me a pallet of boxes. Do you know what they were? Computer boxes with the logo on the side!'

When the boxes had arrived from the island, free gratis on the local ferry, I rang to thank Josephine for all the stuff. 'Thanks for all the boxes. It was great to get it all boxed and ready to go. We took it straight to Shannon to cargo and it is all set. We just have to do the airway bills now and that's it. Oh, and by the way, thanks for the two washing-machines. We weren't expecting them. They'll be a great help!'

'What two washing machines? I didn't send any washing machines?

'Well we got two of them, they're here ready to go to Belarus by air'.

'They must be belonging to someone on the island. Get them back!'

'Taxi! Follow that plane!'

However the aid went, there was always the concern that it was not getting through. Maybe some of it was being stolen along the way. Perhaps customs people were pilfering a little. Perhaps people in the orphanages would help themselves to some of the stuff. Everything has to be counted before being released for use by customs in Belarus. This is a huge task. And I am sure that some stuff we sent went missing. But as Teresa said, 'Sure, as long as somebody who needed it got it, what matter?' And wasn't she right! We have more than we need over here and in our effort to give it away, what matter if some of it went slightly astray and people whom we had not included became part of the deal. All well, as long as the children got their fair share.

A forty-foot truck takes a huge amount of filling and lots of hard work. There is an art in packing a truck and we have become relatively expert in a short space of time. Weights must be balanced over the axles. No space must be left empty as a truck costs a lot to send. It is great to have a good man like Ray on the fork-lift to keep things going. It is also vital to have a really good packer in the truck who will see that every corner is filled and no loose space, no empty holes. This is essential as a truck may cost up to five thousand dollars to send across Europe! Ger O'Connell was always great as the truck was being filled and he pumped sweat in ensuring that not one square inch was left unused. No chance of squeezing anything – or anyone – into the truck after Ger had been involved in the packing. His expertise was rivalled only by James Honan who would pack the inside of a toilet-roll in order to get full value aboard the trucks. Ned and Jim were also great and it was important to have good men when loading, especially when it came to linoleum. This was agony! Tons of detergent, bags of flour, new toilet bowls and cisterns – all were easy compared to lino. Big, heavy, awkward and long. This was the real test. At least in loading the roll, we had the use of a fork-lift. But what would we do in Cherven and Goradishche in trying to unload them. And me with my bad back!

Actually when the trucks did arrive in Goradishche, it didn't turn out too badly. We emptied truck number one in twenty minutes, thanks to the help of all the bigger boys and girls from the orphanage. The second truck was a little slower. The PVC was no real trouble as it was light. The boxes of shampoo and detergent, the soaps and clothes, the wheelchairs and toiletries, all were no trouble. The rolls of linoleum without a fork-lift were also fairly easy as we had a horse of a man in Volodya. He caught one end, pushed it back the truck and fecked it off down on the ground. Then six lads working together put ropes under it and hauled it away to the store. No problem! But then came the tins of paint which we decided to pass along in a chain-line from the front of the truck to the back. All well until one tin of green was let fall and spilt out all over the floor. Next came a bag of burst flour which meant we all ended up sweaty, smelly and covered in a sticky green muck as we continued to offload all the remaining goods.

Back at the flat, later, joy of joys, there was no hot water! My poor back! Sure, no-one knows what I have suffered with it!

All in all, the humanitarian aid shipments have been a great success. We have solved the clothes problem for all the children. We have put in new toilets and showers and have covered all the units with new linoleum. This small part of the work greatly lifts morale. It is so much nicer to work in a nice environment. So much nicer to live there! It sure beats a dull, dreary room. It is good to have somewhere nice to face each day when there may not be too much to be happy about generally. There is great satisfaction in seeing the effect these goods, mostly donated by Irish people, are having. There is great satisfaction in being wrecked tired when a load had just been filled. We have happy memories of sitting at the side of the street near Cullinan's yard at one o'clock in the morning sucking Franco's fried chicken and chewing chips, hot and sweaty but delighted that the truck is filled, ready for off, ready to make a difference to children in a far distant orphanage, far away across many frontiers. It is good

to sit and reflect and listen to Liam Grant's dry wit. Another
load ready. Let's go!

We are thankful to everyone for making it all possible.
Sending much needed aid is one part of the solution. Another is
to try to lift morale. To let the workers who earn forty dollars a
month for working in these extreme situations know that we
care about them also was another part of our approach. We tried
to understand what it must be like to work a twelve hour day
and then face home wondering what to give one's own child to
eat. It could not be an easy life! It was Frances who suggested
that it would be good to give the workers in the orphanage a
small bonus to let them know how we appreciated how difficult
things are for them. We can recall ourselves getting a letter from
overseas and the value and the joy of a few dollars arriving unexpectedly. So, all the workers got a little bonus in the summer.
Each and everyone without exception was given a small stipend.
We wished it could be more but when there are two hundred
and fifty workers it is hard to stretch our funds. But yet it told
people that we were trying our best and would continue to do so
and that we appreciated their efforts also in a very difficult situation.

Washing machines and drying machines were by now in-
stalled. Playground equipment had begun to be set up so that
the children will have more than the one swing between them.
New pots and pans for the kitchen. New sauna for the children
in the winter. Wallpaper for every room and new linoleum on
the floors. It is beginning to make a difference in Cherven. We
have made the food situation better and have been able to provide pampers for the children. We arranged for terry nappies
but the women were reluctant to use them as they felt that these
new nappies were too good to use. They saved them and used
them as towels instead.

When the trucks go by road, we follow by air and arrive to
help sorting out the documents, to help unload the trucks and to
see that everything has arrived safely. There are always complications. Things like certain customs deciding that they needed
every item of clothing counted, segregated and de-loused at a
special high temperature before allowing anything through.
And we with a truck full at that stage! There is the story of one of

our friends who also sends lorry loads to Belarus. When he arrived at a certain border he was short one document when
checked at the customs office.

'Go out,' he said to his fellow driver, 'and bring in that document.'

'What?'

'Go out and bring in that document!'

'We haven't got that document,' he whispers back.

'Go out and get it!'

So out he went. Got some headed paper. Then he wrote out
whatever was needed on the page. Put a pound coin on it, hit it a
wallop with a hammer to show it had a proper seal. Then signed
it C. J. Haughey and brought it back in. No problem. All documents present and correct! Please pass through!

So much for the power of CJH!

It was Maura who saw to the filling of the trucks and the un-
loading in Belarus. This is a big job in Ireland and takes time in
Belarus as well. Usually documents are slow at customs, usually
there are delays for various reasons but eventually the truck gets
emptied. Our one instruction to the driver before he leaves
Shannon is 'don't bring it back'. So, finally satisfied that all was
accomplished in Belarus, it bothered Maura when she realised
that the truck might be going home empty. So Maura asked
Liam Grant, the driver, if he would mind bringing back a rare
breed of dog for her. I told her not to ask him but she asked him.
I told her what he'd say and he said it.

'Liam , would you mind bringing back a pug dog for me, on
the truck?

'I'll feck yourself and your dog into the English Channel',
said Liam. And he would!

So, we have the satisfaction of knowing that we are making a
difference for the children in Cherven. The visits to Ireland for
rest, medical care and recuperation are all of great benefit to the
children. The delivery of much-needed basic necessities is also
making a difference. The presence there of regular groups of
volunteers is also having a positive effect. There is much still to
be done but at least a good start has been made. Things are moving in the right direction.

Cherven is just one of our projects. We have already put huge time, finance and effort into making it a better place for the children there. We will continue as long as we have the support and the funds to do so. It is hard work along with everything else but so much of this story is emotional that it is good to have pure physical hard work to do at times. It keep donkey plodding along at peace.

CHAPTER FOURTEEN

Mothers in Minsk

Not all children in Belarus end up in orphanages. Not all handicapped children are sent away to be looked after by the state. There are people who make the effort to keep their child at home. For such parents, there is often little state support. The child is at home in a loving environment but that may be all. No school. No facilities. No break for the mother – and in many cases it is the mother who is left when a handicapped child is born. There is no chance to get a break, to get the shopping done, to have a few free hours or to find some small job to supplement whatever income there is.

Again, a few years ago we were lucky enough to meet up with a few of these good parents, parents who were desperately trying to find some means to enable them to open a school, a centre for their children. The group was organised by Olga and Tamara, two mothers with a special-needs child. They went around Minsk putting together the names and addresses of families with a handicapped child. I have visited some of the flats in Minsk with them. We saw together the conditions under which some people live. Yes, there are those who have a flat with hot water and proper facilities. But there are also those who have very primitive conditions. This is extremely difficult where the child is bedridden and doubly incontinent. We visited one woman who lives in a small one-room wooden shack with her two children, one a special needs child who cannot be left alone. In this room all of life is lived. In this room there is no privacy of any kind for anyone, not even for one's thoughts.

We visited another very sad case, this time in a flat. Here we met an elderly woman trying to mind her handicapped son who had partnered a handicapped woman to give birth to another handicapped child. This was one of the saddest situations. For the mother, the future was a dark place where there was no hope. In another flat, a large girl lay on a bed where she has been for years, her mother being unable to bring her down the several flights of stairs as she has no wheelchair and no possibility of getting one. Some of the problems are huge. But some are small and could easily be solved. That is one of the saddest things. A wheelchair here, a few dollars there and life could be so much better for so many people in so many ways.

We have put a huge amount of effort and energy into making the orphanages better places for the children there. We have been trying to make them suitable places where people can live and work. There is a sense though in which we consider that this is the wrong way to go into the future. Under the Communist system, big was good and bigger was better. We have been in orphanages for children and adults where over four hundred people are crowded with very basic conditions. The old people's asylums are very sad places. We realised that the way forward is to undo all we have done in a sense, to begin trying to bring an end to these large institutions. It is time to begin to make small houses where children can live in a family situation. It is time to build homes for all those children who are categorised under the former Soviet system as oligophrenic, idiot or imbecile. Those are the categories. Many, many children are well capable of living a normal life. Many many more are well capable of living a life with just a little direction. This is what we want to bring about. This has to be one of our aims. To break up the monolithic system where so much humanity is crowded into huge institutions and people lose their identity. There has to be a way to end this, to get people out of the system.

With this in mind we were happy to help out with setting up a day centre in Minsk for Olga and Tamara and their families and children. They had managed to get permission to use a part of a discarded kindergarten to set up a place for their own children. All they needed was money. We were able to provide that. My advice to Olga and Tamara was advice once given to me by Brother Con Leen, a beautiful man who said once, 'Begin it, someone else will finish it, but always begin it.' So Olga and Tamara began work. At first a group of ten children began in the centre. Parents came along to give a hand. Each day, one parent would arrive with food for the children – whatever she could manage to supply from her own resources. Bit by bit the place began to take shape. Tables were brought in. Tax Revenue chairs arrived on our truck thanks to the Limerick office. Paint and paper, jigsaws and puzzles. Slowly it began to take place. A teacher was found who would work with the children. Then a music teacher. Then a physiotherapist with a few hours to spare. We supported this all along with funding.

Later a second group opened up in a second room. Now twenty-two children had the chance of a schooling. Twenty-two families had the opportunity to bring their child to school. Twenty-two mothers had time to shop, to do a few hours work, a chance to rest, knowing that their child was in a safe place.

Back in Cherven in group four a new boy had arrived. A little black boy. It was most unusual to see a coloured boy in the orphanages. This little boy named Ilya is the son of an art student who lives in Minsk and who could not possibly keep him at home as she has no-one to mind him while she is at classes. Ilya is deaf and there is little chance that anything can be done to improve this situation. However, thanks to having opened the Day Centre in Minsk we were at least able to have him transferred there and his mother could take him home in the evenings. Another child reunited with his mother, a mother who loves him very much.

Later, this story became complicated as racial prejudice raised its ugly head and people living in the block of flats decided they didn't want a black boy sharing the building with them. Not even his cute black curls or his impish smile could convince them otherwise. At present, Ilya and his mother have been taken in by the mother of another of the children at the day centre. They share their days and their homes. Pavil, this other boy, is a beautiful artist. He paints every day. Beautiful pictures. He is a bright eyed, happy child who loves painting. He paints with his left foot. It is the only part of his body which will obey his commands. He has a little command over his head and can indicate with his eyes what he wants. The Day Centre is papered with his paintings. He is beautiful.

I get a chance to spend a little time in the centre sometimes. This is a time to be with the children and to see the happy bustle of excitement that goes on there. I have seen the children crying when it is time to go home. They just want to stay at school and be busy doing things. It is a happy place. Every day during the holidays the children ask if it is a school day. Is it the first of September yet? They love going there. One of the big boys there has a very broken and twisted body. A body that often refuses to obey the commands of his brain. Yet, Vita can sit up and with great effort he can talk. He loves coming to the centre ever day. He said, 'When I came to the centre, it was the first time I realised that I am human, that I am a person'.

Sometimes the children have outings. Once we brought them to the circus. The Minsk Circus is famous. It has a special build-ing, with tiered seating rising all round the centre ring. A spe-cially designed circus building. I have been there to hear other children comment on seeing our children, 'here come the clowns'. This is where they are at. It is upsetting for the parents but I tell them they must keep at it. The must keep bringing their children into the open, into the streets, into places where every-one else goes. They must do this. Their children have this right too.

Andrei is another very special little boy. I spent over an hour with him one morning. He has no control over his body. He just lies there. But his eyes are alive. I know nothing about cerebral palsy in children but maybe I know a little about children. I spent some time with him, making faces, talking, playing. First, we rattled some cymbals. Then again. After a while his eyes fol-lowed the noise. I rattled when he looked. Then I pretended to put my finger in his mouth and pretended that he bit me and that it hurt. I made imaginary faces of pain. Andrei smiled. We repeated this over and over. Each time he smiled. His body shook on the couch where he lay and he chortled silently within himself. I kept at my foolacting and then Andrei laughed. Like Sergei at home. A beautiful chuckle of a laugh. Heads turned to watch. To hear. It is beautiful to hear a child laugh. It was beauti-ful to hear Andrei. Just beautiful.

To keep this centre going requires money and there was al-ways the chance that the government would withdraw permis-sion and take over the building again. The best solution was to buy a house that they could use as their own, that would be theirs as a centre forever. A gang of lawyers and solicitors walking and running from Westport to Galway was how this was mainly funded. Thanks to Ger and Rose Mary who had come to visit Belarus with us, this project took off. A house was bought in Minsk which would become the new day centre. There was even money for a minibus to ferry the children to and from school each day.

Olga and Tamara have since gone on and with the help of their menfolk have done marvellous work about this centre. There now stands beside the house a new workshop where the children will have the chance to learn new skills. The grounds have been made children-friendly and wheelchair accessible. It is the beginning of something great. We have made the beginning. Someone will finish it.

Olga and Tamara visited the orphanage in Cherven with me once. Olga said: 'I never thought I would see a thin Down's Syndrome child.' Olga's daughter, the beautiful Vera, is a Down's. Tamara was in tears as she said: 'If we let our children go to the orphanage, they would be like this. We will never let them go!'

Family is the best place for children. We try to make that happen. Now we will try to raise funds to keep this centre going and to get a flat for Ilya and his lovely Mamma. It is a privilege to be part of this story. Like Vita, it makes us all feel a little more human, a little more in touch with the important and the vital. Thank God.

CHAPTER FIFTEEN

Little ones who believe in me

On our summer 2000 visit to Belarus, we had twenty-six volunteers spending their annual vacation time working in the orphanages. This was one of the now regular trips. The work involved the usual round of activities – cleaning and washing the children, changing them into clean nappies and clean clothes. It involved gentle massage of the children, many of whom have severe constrictions, twisted limbs and spasm. A little daily massage of the limbs does great in easing the tightness of the limbs and we feel sure that with proper care many of these children could in fact actually walk. Vika is one of these children. If she had not been brought to Ireland and cared for she would have died. If we hadn't insisted on proper care for her she would have been left in a bed always. Now she is up and about, very active and mobile and will have a different life by simple virtue of the fact that she can walk.

This is the aim then, to give as many as possible the opportunity to walk. Max had one month in Ireland. He went from someone without any wish for life to someone who actually gets out of his bed and bums his way about, even venturing outdoors on his bum when managing to give the workers the slip. For them, this is of course an extra worry. For Max it is the first major statement in the only way he can that he will not be left in bed and forgotten. We hope to continue this work with Max in Ireland in the coming months. There is also Vitalic, Olga, Andrei, Kristina and Alosha.

And there is Jenka. Jenka Zelski is another one of the special children from Group Four in Cherven. Another unwanted child. Another rejected by his mother. Another unaccounted father. Jenka has Hurler's Syndrome which is slowly taking his life. It is too late to do anything for him except wrap him in the love, which Martina brought to him, and enfold him in the continued love of Tina and Jim in Killaloe. There is only one end to Jenka's story. He will not get better. Most children with Hurler's Syndrome die in their second decade, many at the age of eight or nine. A fairly simple bone-marrow operation while a baby can have a huge effect in making life better. For Jenka this did not happen. Now it is too late. What will happen when Jenka does die is unknown to us. Jim and Tina very much want him to remain here in Ireland where they can visit his grave and talk to him. For Jenka it may soon be a release to have his spirit freed from the body in which it now struggles for breath. It may be a relief to pass on. He has spread his special love and joy, his bright alertness and his beautiful personality all over those who have met him. He has been treated like royalty by the beautiful nurses in Crumlin children's hospital. He has left his mark.

Side by side with coping with the trauma, the joy and the work that is going on and is being done by wonderful families here in Ireland is the work which has to be ongoing in Belarus. We have done five hard years since first visiting Cherven. There are changes. We are making progress. The place is cleaner and brighter. The staff are co-operative and helpful in the main. The new Director in each orphanage is really trying to make a difference. This means trying to change attitudes in a system which doesn't value handicapped children. We live in the fear that the work we do will help children for a while and then that they will have improved and be left in a worse situation than if we had not begun. We live in the fear that many of these children will die when they leave their present orphanage and go to an asylum for adults. Adult mental asylums in any country probably are not great. In a country with poor economics and an indifferent attitude the situation is all the worse.

This was confirmed for us when we were there in July. Group Thirteen is one of the groups we love the most. It has about twenty-two teenage boys of varying ages and disabilities. It is the unit for the psychiatric, the unwanted, the end of the line. So many of us love this group. It frightened me big time on my first visit. I had never seen so much rocking, so many shaved heads, so much neglect, so much empty room, so much control, in all my life. I wondered would they eat me, bite me, attack me. They sat and rocked and ate the sweets, papers and all. My stupidity in bringing wrapped sweets!

In August a twenty-two year old boy died. He had lived his recent years sitting perched like a wet hen on the seat of a wheelchair. His face read pain. He huddled. He waited. Huddled. He responded to sweets. The other psychiatric, so-called oligophrenic boys always made sure that everyone got sweets. They looked after one another. They looked after him. They made sure he got his share. They shared. Part of this sharing was to give me some of the chewing gum they were chewing. They chewed it and then put some in my mouth. I chewed it and begged forgiveness for my wanting to reject. They cared for this boy, Vova.

Vova was rejected when he was born. He had twenty-two years in an institution, let's not call it living. He died. I went down to group thirteen when I heard he had died. I was amazed as I did not realise he was that ill. The women said they knew nothing about a boy dying. I showed them his bed and asked about the boy who died. They said they knew nothing. I thought it was my bad Russian. The interpreter came with me. He offered our condolences on the death of a boy. The old lady laughed. He repeated in case there was some misunderstanding. She laughed out loudly again. I was shocked. Our interpreter was ashamed, ashamed to be part of this country, of this system, to be there to see how much the Irish group were trying to do and then to see this reaction at the death of a young man. She laughed. Again, it is one of these moments which strikes the imagination and settles there, like a living thing. A young man died. The lady in charge laughed.

Vova was rejected at birth. He was unloved and unwanted all his life. He died for some reason that we do not know. Perhaps it was cancer. Perhaps ulcers. Maybe it was starvation. Maybe he just wanted to go. His carer, his minder, laughed at his death. Next door, group twelve didn't even know. A young man had died right beside them and it didn't make the news. It was not reported. Not spoken about. It didn't matter. No ceremony. No sorrow. Bye bye, nice knowing you! None of that.

Frances and I decided to go to the graveyard, to see where they ended up, these little children. These unwanted. It wasn't far away. In a beautiful sylvan setting, the white larch reaching tall to the sky, the graveyard looked not bad as we arrived. We had to go off the main track to find where the little children were buried. It was round the back – somewhere. Maybe here? Maybe here? We searched and searched. Small graves, sometimes in rows of six or seven; sometimes alone, bumped up from the ground. Maybe this was the spot. There was no name, no date of birth, no recognition of having passed this way one little while and then no more. There were bumps on the earth. We walked over them and tried to make out any scratches, any possible writing. It was impossible. Here is one with a date. Age seven. Age five here. Age eleven. Maybe this is it? Maybe it is. We walked over them again, this time praying for the little souls, praying forgiveness that we had let them pass through this life as unwanted children, pass through to death as unwanted, pass into the earth in an unmarked spot at the back end of a cemetery. We prayed for help to make this world a place fit for children, a place of love, a place of hope. We simply prayed and tried to let them know that we had heard them call, even if too late for them and for us. We heard but in a wood darkly, dimly, poorly, too late. Simply too late.

As we left, a herd of about one hundred cows from the local collective farm were making their way through the forest, walking over the graves of the children.

CHAPTER SIXTEEN

Jenka's Funeral

'Liam. I've just had a phonecall from Tina. Jenka is not well at all, the little angel.'

It was Teresa on the line. Word had come through that Jenka was finally slowing down, on the last stages of his journey. His Hurler's Syndrome was beginning to take its toll. He had been to hospital for a hernia operation but it would have been too much to put him through, as his life expectancy was so limited. There was no guarantee he would come back from the anaesthetic. So, Jim and Tina brought him home to Killestry, near Killaloe and watched and waited on his last days. We went to visit him and saw how difficult it was for him to breathe. How difficult it was on his heart to keep on making such an effort. The oxygen machine provided some relief but it would not be too long. He sat on Jim's lap and tried to find a position of ease, a degree of comfort.

We always knew there could be only one outcome to Jenka's condition. He would die. Now, we had to prepare. He is not adopted. He is from Belarus and although he has been here a long time, would the powers that be allow him to remain here, to be buried here? We had to begin to make remote preparations. First, contact Martin in Belavia Airline office to check were there tickets available at short notice if Jenka dies. Yes, no problem. Then, inform the Belarus Embassy in London that there is the serious possibility that a Belarusian child will die here. What is the procedure? Could he be allowed to stay here for burial? Luckily Mr Dzemidkov is a good man and a friend. Approachable.

Then, the horrible part! If he has to go back, how do we do it?

Get on to Helen in Elite Kamino. She will know the procedure. 'Yes, we can arrange the documents. We have done it before to other countries. Unfortunately, a coffin goes as a piece of cargo. I know it sounds awful but that it how it is. We will need to know the weight of the coffin and there are certain documents to be done – death cert., coroner's report. The undertakers will know about those. They will probably have done them before. Let me know. I will make remote enquiries from the freight people.'

Jenka died just after one o'clock in the morning on 11 September 2002. Teresa had got the early morning call and was at the monastery door to wake me up with the news.

'Liam, Jenka is gone.'

So began one of the busiest and most emotional few days ever. Trying to make all the final arrangements, discussing with the Belarus Embassy in London. Contact with the Irish Embassy in Moscow. Waiting in hope that the authorities would let Jenka be buried here. Yet having to have everything ready in case they didn't.

Jenka was removed to Killaloe Church on the edge of beautiful Lough Derg on the Thursday evening. There was no hearse. Jim and Tina didn't want it. We brought him in Teresa's van, the small white coffin on the middle seat, Tina in the front and Jim and Martina squashed in at the back. The church was crowded with so many people who have been touched by Jenka and his Belarusian friends. A beautiful ceremony for a beautiful child. I am struck by the amount of people in attendance. Compared to what would have happened had Jenka died in Belarus, in the orphanage. I am struck by the memory of the phonecall when I was in southern Belarus when Maria was looking for another Liam. It was that contact which lead to Cherven Oprhanage which lead to Jenka being here which lead to this scene of grieving and support.

After Mass I checked for messages on my answering machine. There was a message from the Belarus Embassy in London. Jenka must go back. Angry at first, Jim and Tina were great. It

must be the right thing to do. It must be what Jenka wants. There
must be a reason for it.

So we confirmed the tickets. Booked freight space for one
small coffin. Informed the Embassies. Informed the orphanage
of arrangements. Got hospital reports of Jenka's condition and
prognosis. Got a doctor's certificate stating reason of death. Got
a coroner's report stating there was no need for the body to be
retained in Ireland due to infection. Made arrangements with
John and Mary Lynch Undertakers to embalm the body, zinc-
line the coffin and arrange delivery on Monday morning to
Shannon Airport. Arrange to pick up the Belarussian Consul
from the Embassy who would seal the coffin and ensure that all
documents were in order.

And so it happened. Hopefully we had remembered everything. And away we went on that Monday morning. Perhaps
still not quite confident that it was the right thing to do but
knowing that it must be so and that there is a reason for everything.

'I want to meet his mother', said Tina. 'I want to thank her for
her generosity.'

They stood on the runway at Minsk International Airport beside the Tupalov waiting for the coffin to be unloaded. It was
cold. I went inside looking for someone to ask what to do. I met
a lovely girl whom I have got to know on my various trips. I
asked what should we do. Where would we get the coffin? She
asked one of the officials in a uniform. A young, pleasant man.
He came to us. I told him the story. By now the coffin was unloaded onto the back of a truck. This good man collected our
passports and ushered us through Passport Control. No queu-
ing. No waiting. Back came our passports. Our luggage was
ready and away we went. I explained to baggage control why
we were here. Everyone was so nice to us. So pleasant, so polite.

The coffin was brought through like a piece of luggage and
placed on the back seat of the bus from the orphanage. Our bags
were placed beside it. Off we went to Cherven. There, they had a
room ready in the Medpunkt Medical Unit. We placed the coffin

there, lit some candles and said a few prayers. In the morning we would collect the priest from Minsk for the funeral and we would send a car for Jenka's mother.

The priest came under his own steam as he had another funeral. He intoned the prayers over the coffin, now laid in the orphanage hall. Then he left. 'You will do the graveyard prayers yourself.' So we sat and waited. Jenka's mother had not yet arrived. The local people said the Rosary in Russian. Jim sang *Angel of God*. We waited. James O'Shea, Irish Consul, sang the Ár nAthair, sean-nós style. Beautifully.

Like a faery form reminiscent of our Celtic past a woman moved through the crowd, Sinéad O'Connor echoing through the roofbeams of my mind. *My young love said to me ...* Arriving late, daughter and son in tow, she made her way through the gathered children to where the coffin of her own son now lay, all the way up to the front. There she sat, beside Jim and Tina, and Martina. Eyes followed her every step, eyes eyed her up and down. Who is she? Why did she come? Why did she reject Jenka? Why didn't she care? Why did she come now? And how young she is!

After a little time for quiet prayer or thought or to recover or whatever it is that went on in her head, I went up to explain who we were, who Martina was, who Jim and Tina were. I said how thankful they were to have had Jenka in Ireland, to have him in their lives. I showed her the photo of Jenka, which they had placed on the top of the coffin. She didn't take it in her hands as I thought she might. She just looked at it. I placed it down near her, at the end of the coffin, and she looked at it and looked at it and kept on looking at it. Seated behind her, her daughter cosseted her younger brother, her young eyes watchful and careful.

I asked the orphanage boys and girls to move out to give the two sides of Jenka's life a small chance to meet and make contact. There was only a little time before removing the remains.

A nod to the director, Victor, and the boys and girls came back in to collect the flowers and bouquets. Out they went with them. Then the big boys and men came in to carry the small coffin out through the crowd, along the corridor, to the right and out the front door. There, the boys and girls were lined up in guard-of-honour style on each side with the flowers still in their arms.

Outside the gate on the road side, the lorry waited, its new carpet covering a fitting place for a coffin. A hand-made cross with Jenka's name lay aslant against the back of the front of the lorry. Beside real mother and daughter and son, followed by Irish parents and Martina, we watched the coffin laid gently on the lorry, ready for his last trip. I eased the family towards the orphanage bus and the crowd of children and adults climbed on, some through the front door, some in the back. James O'Shea was there with Katya from Minsk and they found seats some-where down the back of the bus where the coffin had rested on its journey from the airport.

'It's great that she came. It means a lot,' said Jim of this woman whom we still hadn't properly met and whose son we were about to bury. 'I'm glad we came back. It's what Jenka wanted. I can see that now.'

For me, this is world-collision stuff. This is what happens when different worlds collide. How this woman could break free from all the bonds which hold her here, how she could face us all through all the crowd on the day of the funeral of her Hurler's Syndrome son – knowing what we must think of her and how we felt she had abandoned, rejected her child because of his obvious handicap – and she could face all this and come here and be with us on the bus as we headed out the road away from the orphanage towards the cemetery. 'It means a lot,' said Jim. It means everything. It means everything! It shatters at a glance my own thoughts on how awful people are who reject their child. It answers without question all the calls from our own good people at home at how awful it is that he had to go back. He had to go back. He needed to go back. Jenka wanted to go back. Back home. He wanted us to meet his mother.

Word begins to whisper-spread that she has five children, four and one fostered. What? She has fostered out another one of her children? As well as Jenka? No! She has four other children and she has taken in another child to foster and they are very poor. School is seven kilometres away from where they live and she has a baby who is just one month old.

I have written how awful it is that parents reject their child. They can do so legally here. Now, I see how awful that I have rejected this woman and so many like her because they gave their child to a state orphanage when in her poverty and her goodness she was raising five others – beautifully. The beam in my own eye. How wrong! How awful! How judgemental! Without ever knowing the real situation. Without ever even asking. I am shattered. Shattered by this quiet hero of a woman, this brave woman who took a strong, courageous, difficult decision for her son. Shattered.

About four or five kilometres out, the graveyard lies on the left side of the road, just past the adult asylum where some of our children now live. The lorry with the coffin takes the left culvert and makes its way along the side of the graveyard. It then takes a left at the end, down towards the place around the back. Misha brings the big bus as far as is possible and we all get out. We slide and shuffle down the bank to the lower level. One of the local Catholic Grannies has come along to help with the ceremony. I have dubbed her 'my girl' and I help her down the slope in her slippers. There is no priest.

Down the back where the children are buried, there are improvements. Thanks to Jenka. The little bumps in the ground, which are the children's graves, have been cleaned and rebuilt. Some have crosses. There is a new fenced-off part for Jenka and for future children who will be buried here. A sign on the fence claims this plot for Cherven children. The fence was painted yesterday. A shade of green. The grave is ready. A beautiful clean grave. A mound of clean sand awaits beside the open grave, smoothed level on top with the handle of a shovel. Three pieces of timber lie across the grave waiting to take the weight of the small coffin.

As there is no priest, we do the prayers ourselves. First, the local ladies take us through their prayers in Russian. My old lady sprinkles holy water on Jenka's coffin. They keen out their song in final farewell.

Then in English with the use of the Christian Brothers Prayer book, I lead the prayers 'at the graveside of a brother'. Jenka who spent some time and a few visits in Ennistymon monastery, is laid to rest in the tradition of the Brothers. The children from the orphanage are gathered round. The grave is under the tall whisperings of several soaring larch in a new patch at the end of the graveyard. Together with the trees and the wind, we unite our prayers for Jenka, for his Irish parents and friends, for his real mother, Sveta, and for his family and friends from the orphanage.

At the end, when he is laid to rest, when the grave is smoothed over, there is a tribute to Jenka's love of music. There is a song. Could a child be sent off more beautifully than when James O'Shea, the Irish Consul from our Embassy in Moscow, sang over the grave, 'Down by the Sally Gardens, my love and I did meet,'? It echoed out and breathed up through the tall white larch as Jenka diddle-diddled his way to heaven. Beautiful.

I choke on the emotion of it all, on the goodness of James and the Killaloe group; on the outpouring of grief in Killaloe before we left. I choke on the sheer amount of paperwork that had to be thought of and prepared. And on the fact that a coffin carrying the remains of a child becomes a 'piece of cargo' when transported by plane. I choke mostly on my certainty of what a 'Jenka's mother' would be – uncaring, drunken, a poor mother. I nearly suffocate when I try to regurgitate from my heart what I had assumed, what I had believed, what I was sure I knew about Jenka's mother. And it was all wrong!

She is young, she is beautiful. She is coping well with more than she needs to. And in my wisdom and understanding of life, I had rejected her just as I felt she had rejected her child. It is only part of the story. A door just a tiny bit ajar. There is a whole world of unknowing out there, a new continent of emotion and family relationships in a former Communist state – all waiting to be heard, to be explored, to be understood. A world glimpsed through a mother who came to the funeral of her son who had died in Ireland.

We brought all the children and adults to the restaurant for a meal, which Raisa, our interpreter, had arranged in the middle of everything else. The children had a really great feed and they were so good. For once, there was plenty of everything for everyone.

Sitting beside Sveta, Jenka's mother, I tried to speak to her, to help her relax and know that however we might have felt we knew we were wrong and were beginning to understand her world a little. She wouldn't eat. She couldn't eat. Couldn't lift her eyes to face this world of strange faces, which she knew was watching her. A sweet biscuit to begin the funeral meal. No! But eventually in her own time she had a little of it. Later, lovely mash and cutlets arrived. She brightened a little and took some. When pork arrived, she had a little of that. I cut it up for her on her plate – most people here don't use knives. I felt so good just to be allowed to cut her meat for her. A sharing. We spoke a little of where she comes from. Of her children. Her one month old baby.

Then, later, as she really hadn't much time before heading for home, we walked with Jim and Tina and Martina back to the orphanage. We sat in group one room and they showed her their album of Jenka's life. They shared some of the stories, the things he liked to do, his socks … They spoke of his illness and condition and that it was good that, in the end, he went fairly quickly and didn't suffer long. They spoke of his abilities, his quickness at understanding even English, how he loved music, his many friends and admirers, the packed church in Killaloe for his funeral.

They thanked her for coming; thanked her for allowing them share her child; thanked her for her generosity in allowing them have Jenka. 'It is I who must thank you,' she said quietly, sadly. 'It is I who must thank you.'

'We have a cow and a pig. And we have hens,' she tells us. 'We are poor people. The baby is just one month old, so I have five to mind'.

Sveta looked through all the photos of Jenka and asked a few questions. They explained who everyone was and when and where the photo was taken. By now her son, Vitalic, was enjoying sweets and his sister, Nastya, was looking on by mother's shoulder. 'You can have whatever photos you want. Just pick any you want,' said Jim. She picked out just one photo of Jenka, sitting cross-legged on a great chair, looking very wonderful.

Soon it was time to go. But time also to invite Jenka's sister, Nastya, to Ireland next summer or at Christmas or whenever suits them, whenever her passport is ready. 'Would you like to come?' A nod, shyly, quietly – but her bright eyes reply a shining yes. 'You'll see the lake and the ocean. We live in a very nice place. You'll see where Jenka lived, where we all live. You'll meet his friends.' And she will come and what a welcome she'll get.

They went home to their small farm, to their house far away from everywhere, in some small village. They went back to the lives they had left this morning, this same day. The same lives. The same day. The same journey back. But nothing, absolutely nothing, will ever be the same again. For any of us. Thanks to Jenka.

CHAPTER SEVENTEEN

The Return with the Children

For some reason for several days, I had been dreading and fearing a call from Belarus. Somehow I knew what was going to happen. It was like this for four days. Then on the Wednesday, the call came. It was the Director of the orphanage. The news was that the children all had to go back. All the children had to return. The order had come through from the Director's boss, a woman in an office in Minsk, the capital of Belarus. The news was clear and stark. The children were to be back in the orphanage by 1 November. Was this because Jenka had died in Ireland and now there was understandable panic? Or was it something else? Yet, surely they understood that Jenka had got three great years of quality living in Ireland, which he would not have got in the orphanage? Was this the reason for calling all of them back? Could we somehow intervene and get them to reconsider? Was there any point? Or would going back show them how well all the children were and help to diffuse whatever fears and concerns there might be? We knew without wanting to know that the situation could not go on like this forever. Handicapped children could not leave one country for another and stay there indefinitely without some real check-ups. We felt we had done whatever we could to keep their authorities informed of the conditions and progress of the children. Yet, there had to be some movement from some side. Now that it had come, it was very unpleasant and emotional to have to deal with it, but deal with it we must.

With plane times they way they were, we would have to go on the following Monday or Monday week, 28 October. After one, two and three years of care and attention we were given just over a week to get organised and return. We felt the change of attitude already when no question was asked about if it suited, if the children were well enough to travel, if the children were in the middle of any programme or if they had any special appointments coming up soon. Simply, they must be back in the orphanage by 1 November!

Back after a week. Back into the orphanage. Into the groups where we had first come across them. Flashbacks in my mind. The smells. The handicap. The greyness. The black-and-white slow-motion stillness of memory opening up in my mind. The memories swept under the carpet of forgetfulness as they were too painful to contemplate now became gaping realities. Memories of how it had been. Too much to remember now at this moment. It was a volcano-rumble of emotion within us. It felt to us that the physical return trip would actually turn back the clock. That all the progress the children had made would be undone and that we would simply find ourselves reliving the situation as it had been. That the children would degenerate before our eyes into what they had been. When we took Sergei from his bed three years earlier, his time clock in that place stopped and he moved on. Now, if we returned would his time-line begin again from where he had been and would the progress made in our time zone fall away? This was the stress, the feeling rumbling within us.

Then the forced consolation as the mind takes over. At least now it is clean and bright. At least now it is painted and papered. Pampers … linoleum … washing machines … Each thought an attempt to try to say that it wouldn't be too bad. That the going back wasn't as awful as it might seem. That the place was now better. But still my mind told me it won't be the same as at home. At home in the hearts of people who have loved these children for so long. In hearts where they were nourished and nurtured. Somewhere, a sear of pain in my mind says that in spite of all we have tried to do, it won't be like home. Yet, I know for many children in Belarus being in an orphanage is better than being with their own parents, at home.

The mind continues clicking into reality. Now time for the practicalities. What to do now? What is next? Better tell all the committee members.

'Anne, I've just got a call from Belarus. All the children are to go back! By 1 November!'

'What? All of them? Even Sergei?'

'Yes. Even Sergei!'

'How will you tell Teresa?'

So word went round to all the committee members. The children are to go back. Then time to tell the families who were caring for the children. Loretto in Dublin with her Olga. Sheila in Wicklow with her Andrei and Krystyna. Caitriona in Dublin with her Alosha. Teresa Kehoe in Wexford with her Vitalic. Marian in Ennis with Max. And Teresa nearby here in Miltown Malbay with Sergei. There are two memories of those phonecalls. Firstly, the deadly shock-silence when I told them the news. Then the double-barrelled question: when and for how long? I could answer the first easily, the children were to be back in the orphanage by 1 November. The second question was more of a lottery. The director hoped things could be sorted out quickly. What does that mean in Belarus? I could give no straight definite answer.

The pain-shock and sense of 'they can't do this to the children after all they have been through' seeped and flowed down the phoneline. It was always the same questions, the same fears, the same thoughts. The same raw love-emotion rising and rising and trying to make itself a barrier against the news. Trying to turn back the tide by dint of sheer refusal to accept what had to be accepted. Women in a dramatic moment of time armed and ready to do battle. Women of Limerick against Cromwell. Amazons. Battlers. Ready to fight now at a moment's notice. From the depths of breaking hearts, the fears of good, gentle people choked its way down the line. And a sense that we may have to do it their way, but we will win. We will stay in there and continue to do what is best for these children. And I still had to tell Teresa about Sergei!

Back into the practical world again. What is next? Phone the Belavia airline company office and check if there are in fact tickets for this trip. We won't be upset if the plane is booked out for evermore. Sort out the children's passports. Who has them? Where are they? Contact the Embassy of Belarus in London to see if they can come up with a reason why this is happening now. Contact the Irish Embassy in Moscow to see if they can intervene at a diplomatic level to help put a quick end to this mad journey. Back in Dublin, contact the Irish Departments of

Foreign Affairs and Justice to see if they have any problem with
the children staying in Ireland or in being granted a re-entry visa
or visa-exemption. And wait then for Teresa to return from her
shopping trip to Ennis to break the news.

As Teresa came in the door downstairs the phone was ringing.

'Come on up, Teresa, I'll just get the phone.' It was Frances
on the line. Ringing from the doctor's surgery.

'Liam, can you come down now and get me and bring me to
the hospital in Ennis. I have to go straight into intensive care
with a suspected heart attack.'

Sweet Jesus! Teresa came into the room at the top of the
stairs. Where to begin? What news?

'Teresa, I have two bad news stories for you. Sergei is to go
back. We got the call this morning. And Frances is at the end of
the line about to have a heart attack. We have to get her to intensive care immediately.'

And that is how poor Teresa heard the news. Two shocks together! No nice cup of tea. No friendly chat leading to the news.
Just wallop! Wallop! No time to think, to analyse. No time even
to panic. Just straight to the car to get Frances and get her safely
on her way to intensive care. Her friend, Teresa O'Shea, had just
caught up with the news and was in the process of carrying out
the trip to Ennis. Later, when we were sure that Frances was settled in, we were able to think about Sergei.

'When does he have to go?'

'On Monday 28th most likely.'

'And I'm heading for Africa on the 26th.'

Teresa had been persuaded to visit her son, Timothy, in the
Turkana Desert in Kenya. He had volunteered for three years
and was nearing the end of his time there. Teresa was going on a
visit to see what he had been up to and to get a small break after
three years constant work looking after Sergei. I was looking forward to minding Sergei over the two weeks while she was away,
with the great help of Breda who hopefully would tend to one
end of Sergei while I wouldn't mind doing the feeding and
grooming! Now, what would Teresa do? Go to Africa? Stay at
home? Cancel one trip and replace it with another?

'Teresa, it is meant to be like this. We are always saying that nothing happens by chance. So with this. It is meant to be like this. Sergei wants it this way. He doesn't want you to have to go back to Belarus. I was going to have Sergei for two weeks anyway. Now, it is just that I will be minding him in Belarus instead of in the monastery.'

And then Teresa, with one of her lines which captures all the fears of all the women who are in this position of losing control of a child whom they love, said:

'But, Liam, if they are unkind to him!'

Like all the women, Teresa felt the fear of knowing a hurt or unkind word done to one we love. Like Teresa, I know Sergei as each of the women knows their child. I know what he wants even though he has no words. I know how he reacts. I know how he asks to be tickled. I understand his sounds. I remember the day he slipped down off his bean bag onto the floor. I know that that evening when I visited him he told me all about it and how he was a little hurt and a little frightened. And I know he settled down happily once I had listened to him. Using his own sound-words, he explained it all. And I knew what he meant.

Each of the parents was in this position, knowing all the little ways, the little signs, being expert in the body-language of their particular child. Now they were fearing that the child would return to the silent world of non-communication where nothing would be understood and where nothing could be made known. Back to a world where nobody might really care. That was the big fear for us all. Of course, we knew that they were not our children, not for evermore. But they were all doing so well. All the time and effort. All the expertise that had brought them to this stage of well-being, would it now be wasted? Would they regress and return to the way they had been? These were our questions. We had just been hoping that things would continue as they were until everything could be sorted out.

Yet, what were we to do? We could defy the call to return and risk causing problems for all the children and for the entire project. We felt we had to return, to comply with the wishes of the authorities in the hope that this would stand to us later on. So, we prepared and those who were free to do so, or who could arrange time off, decided to travel back with their children in the hope and expectation that there would be a quick turnabout.

Everyone was desperately trying to believe that the Belarus authorities would look at, view, inspect the children. Then they would be satisfied that all was well. Then they would do the documentation to allow the children to return to Ireland to recommence the programmes that had so rudely been interrupted. All would be well! That was our hope. That is what we clung onto. Some hope as it turned out! Some belief!

On Saturday, Teresa was to go to Africa. With her daughter, Angela, we took her to the airport in Shannon. Sergei was with us as she wanted him with her to the last moment, as long as possible. Not only had Teresa packed her own bags but Sergei's bags were at home in his room waiting for his trip on Monday. We went upstairs and had a coffee and we waited. Waited for the call for Teresa's flight, the call which would separate herself and Sergei for who knows how long. Time for her to go. Time to say goodbye. First, hugs and kisses for us, then for her little darling. At the desk, Teresa showed her boarding-card. The man on duty is a friend and would have allowed us through with her. But no! One goodbye at an airport is enough because it may be goodbye forever. Who knows? 'Goodbye darling' and she hugged him. And as she walked through to departures, Teresa did not look back because she could not look back.

The following Monday morning, I loaded the van with all our stuff for the journey, bags, boxes and suitcases. On top was Sergei's prayer-teddy which had come from America. Squeeze his middle and a baby voice prays:

Before I lay me down to sleep
I give the Lord my soul to keep
The angels watch me in the night
Until I wake in morning light. Amen.

Loretto had spent the night in the monastery with her Olga and was already loaded and ready for the road. Sergei had wakened and been changed and fed. He was washed and dressed with his new clothes specially for the journey. Now he was ready in his wheelchair and it was time to go. We loaded him into the minivan and packed more of the luggage around him. Time to lock up the house and set off. Frances home from intensive care sat in beside me. 'Let's go.' I turned the key. The van was dead. Not a glimmer of life. It just will not start. The van which had brought

Sergei so faithfully and carefully all over the place for all his appointments and meetings simply will not work this morning of all mornings. It refuses to start. Refuses to take Sergei on this particular journey to the airport and back to the orphanage. It is the first time the van has not worked when we needed it.

'Heart attack or no heart attack, Frances we need you now.' So we emptied everything from the van and repacked everything into two cars. Sergei was stretched on the reclining front-seat of my car. Frances had all the boxes and cases in her car. You get a lot of sympathy from us after a suspected heart-attack! Off we went. Through Ennis, then onto the new road bypass of Newmarket. A part of me wanted to keep left, not to take the turn to Shannon and just keep on driving, myself and Sergei. Heading off wherever the road would bring us. So what if we didn't make the plane? Ever! I spoke to Sergei on the way. Reminded him of how much we loved him, of how much Teresa loved him. Told him he wasn't ever to forget any of the love we had for him. I thanked him for all he had brought into our lives. We hoped together that all would be well and that we would be back again as soon as Teresa would be back from Africa.

Organised chaos perfectly describes what was happening at the airport. From check-in desk number sixteen, our group of children and women plus the group heading for Goradishche stretched in never-ending line across the terminal, all the way. Trolley convoy of boxes and bags, convoy of wheelchairs and buggies. All stretched out in line and being eaten up slowly by check-in desk sixteen. The group of women heading for Goradishche orphanage with Pat were here also, many for the first time heading to Belarus. For them there was the excitement of adventure, something new, a world or even a window opening up in a foreign dreamed-of place. For other women, there was horror and tears. They had been before and knew what the children were heading back to. Emotional melting-pot. Photographers and journalists were interested in the story and were eager for photos and interviews. My heart was actually heavy with what these children and women had gone through since they had become involved, since they had become interested in working with the children of the orphanage. What had we put them all through? Was it worth it? It is great that these people care so much about the children but is it fair to put any of them through all of this? Would it have been better to do nothing? Not to feel the pain? Not to cry over this situation? No! This is what the real world is made of. Love until it hurts.

The journalists came to hear the story. Were we hopeful? We had to be hopeful. Sometimes it is all we have. Hope. But my heart is heavy. Photos please. Yes. With Sergei. With the children. This is how they were when they arrived. These are the photos.

'Liam, can I have a photo presenting you with this cheque which we raised in Kildare?'

It was Pat Flaherty and Mary Ryan who had done Trojan work over the past while raising money for the project. Now turn and smile for their happy cameras. Back to heartbreak with the journalists. Then Martina Ward from Galway:

'Can we have a photo too presenting this cheque which we raised through a sponsored soccer game?' I think is what she said. More smiles and happy photos. Then back to the reality of the return journey. Emotional seesaw. This is what it will be like over the next while, all the time we are in Belarus. It will be good news, bad news. Believe nothing, is what I told the women. When you hear good news, don't get excited. When you hear bad news, don't get depressed. All will work our. Everything will seem fine, then everything will seem awful. Don't get upset by it as it will be very emotional all the time.

Thanks to Phillip and Tommy and friends, cars are taken away and parked safely. Boxes and bags are checked through. Pat sorts out all the tickets, passports and boarding passes. Then we are called to board. No time for regrets. No time for turning back. No time even for duty-free. Getting a handicapped child with a wheelchair onto a plane is horrendously difficult. Add to that the hand-luggage, feed bottles and pampers plus all the bits and pieces needed for a child on a long journey and it becomes a nightmare.

Leaving the terminal building, the actual physical motion of walking from the building was like forcing oneself to walk into a fire or through a brick wall. All the natural instincts which have developed and evolved in us to protect our young, those we love, had to be fought against. These natural responses had to be overcome in order to take that walk out onto the runway, in order to comply with the regulations of a foreign, sovereign state which had issued the order for the children to return. Some deep part of me believes strongly that it was actually in essence wrong to go back with these children. It was not the right thing to do for them. Another more compliant part sees a bigger picture where other children wait in need and this part says we had to go back. It was the only real option. We had to comply. We had to obey the authorities, yet knowing, as we did, that this is about rules and regulations and not about children. Not about these children at all. Nobody actually wants these children back. Nobody actually wants these children. Somebody somewhere wants a rule kept. Yet there are surely times when justice demands the breaking of an odd rule or regulation.

Out we went onto the runway. Somewhere at the bottom of the steps to the aeroplane a kind man offered help. Somehow we got all the children on board. First the child. Then go back down for the hand-luggage. Leave the wheelchair at the bottom of the steps and they will look after it. For Sheila it was two trips for each child. I was strapping in Sergei as Sheila arrived exhausted and crying with Andrei. Then back and repeat the process with Krystyna. The sheer physical exhaustion, the sheer pain, the sheer fear of what was ahead for these children. It is wrong. It is simply wrong. Wrong to put a woman like Sheila who spends her life caring for medically-fragile, dying children through this. It is wrong. And as I glimpse her tears and fears, I feel shame. Is there a better human being in the world than Sheila, and to put her through this! And for what?

In Minsk Airport, we do the same again in reverse. Wheelchair off. Bags or child first? Leave the bags? Leave the child? Fox, goose, bag of corn! Can I leave the child while I'm getting the bags? Can I leave the bags while I'm getting the child? On the runway? Eventually we get to the terminal building. Declaration forms are filled out. Passport control. The inevitable wait for the luggage and the lack of trolleys. Then the inspection of all we had brought. Luckily, a friend, Sasha works in this area and he was a great help in getting us through without too much bother as did Tatiana, a friend who works in customs.

The big bus from Cherven Orphanage was waiting to meet us outside. With all our luggage there was hardly room for the children and ourselves. But we managed to squeeze in. The Director met us warmly. Emotion was still dripping from everyone as we headed off on that journey. People were quiet, not knowing, just hoping that all would be well once we got settled. The question now on everyone's mind is will they allow us stay with the children or will the children be sent straight back to the units? Suffice it to say that eventually our women and children were left together. Loretto and Olga shared with Sheila and Andrei and Krystyna. Max was with Viv in room one where Theresa and Vitalic also shared with Yula and her Northern Ireland Mammy, Carmel. Caitriona was in another room with her Alosha and there was a bed there also for Sergei. I stayed in our little house down the street, and so at least we had arrived.

Following the trauma of the journey and the entrance into the high heat of the orphanage, the children had slight temperatures. They were all dosed! The next two days saw them being blood-tested, nose-swabbed and bum-swabbed. The almost hostile intrusion onto the lives of the children was very offensive and upsetting. It is not so much what was done but the manner in which tests are carried out that is most difficult to accept. Of course, we understood that checks had to be made in case of infection but nobody asked any questions about how they were, what they had been through, if they were on any treatments or medications. The system simply took over and the children were swabbed, tested and sedated as thought necessary, much to the chagrin and horror of our Irish women who know these children so well and recognise when there is anything up with them.

Bit by bit a rhythm of feeding and meetings took shape. Make Sergei his vegetable mix every morning. Make bottles of porridge for evening. In between, several meetings were held in Minsk with several departments and Ministries. It would have been nice to have had time to spend with Sergei each day apart from feeding times but demands meant I had to feed him and leave and go to Minsk in the hope of meeting someone who could bring this siege to an end. Someone who could make a decision and allow the children back to Ireland to continue their various health and educational programmes. We had a few names, a few departments which we hoped would help. We set out in the hope that there would be a quick resolution. That there would be a way back home quickly. What simple, foolish people we are!

The lady in charge of affairs for the handicapped children in this area of Belarus was one of the good people I managed to meet. I had met her on a previous trip and she told me then that if I had any problems with the Director of Cherven I was to come to her. I had already phoned her from Ireland and so headed to her office in the hope of a pleasant meeting. I found her office and waited in the hope that she could fit me in for a few minutes.

'You must understand, Gospodin Liam, should I call you Liam, yes Liam, that our laws are not ready. It is necessary to have new laws and regulations before the children are allowed to travel.

'When do you think that legislation might be in place?'

'It is impossible to say. Maybe three months.'

'You must understand that these children are in the middle of various programmes of health and development. Here, look at these photos. This is how the children were. This is how they are now. Surely, they can continue their programmes abroad until legislation is in place and then we will bring them back again as you wish.'

'You must understand, Liam, that in our country it takes time.'

'These children don't have time. And it is not just these children. There are other children in Cherven whom we want to take to Ireland also. If they do not go they will die. They don't have three months.'

Then she looked at the photos and after some moments said:

'Maybe it could be done quicker.'

Then she looked at her assistant, they exchanged glances and my time was up.

Meanwhile life was going on all about us. Sergei at this time was in the isolation unit in one of the rooms. A new boy was brought in and dropped off by his mother. We don't know why she did this at this particular time after several years of looking after the child. He is another Sasha. A beautiful blond Down's

Syndrome child. He can dress himself and feed himself. He doesn't talk but does communicate with his own sounds. He did his driving a car sounds and made shapes with his hands. Then he pointed to the window and said: 'du du du Mama.' He knew that Mama was gone home in the car. In the morning he went in to Caitriona, pointed to his watch and to the brightness in the windows. Time to get up! He woke Sergei and Alosha. Later, when I was feeding Sergei he came and stroked his face and kissed his forehead. When this Sasha coughs he politely puts his little fist to his mouth. After a few days waiting for Mama, he came and sat on my lap, put his arms about my neck and cried for du du du Mama. The medical report which accompanied Sasha to the orphanage, describes him as 'Down's Syndrome, oligophrenic to the degree of imbecility'. In the system here, this beautiful child will always be an imbecile.

All the while we had been in touch with the various Ministries which we thought might be able to help us to get some momentum on getting the children home again – Humanitarian Aid, Health and the Department of Social Affairs. In a moment of great stress for us and in a measure of great support, James O'Shea, Consul from the Irish Embassy in Moscow arrived to take up the cudgel on behalf of these children and to present a diplomatic offensive to the cause. An official letter was thus lodged with the Department of Foreign Affairs in Minsk seeking their help in sorting out the situation. The children were lost somewhere in the quagmire of the labyrinth of paperwork. All the while my mind regurgitates the thought:

'In all of this, the one thing that has puzzled me is why am I here on this side of the desk begging you for permission to take these children to Ireland for care? Why am I here begging you to allow us pay extra workers to help these children? You are the official responsible to all these children. You have seen what we have achieved. Why are you not the one begging us to take more of the children and help them? Why?'

The answer was always the same.

'These are our children. We need to draw up new rules and regulations before we can allow any children from the orphanages for handicapped children to travel abroad. Maybe in a month. Maybe in three months. It needs new legislation. When this is done, then we will do the paperwork. Until then, the children must remain here.'

Then the bombshell.

'These are our children. You may have fifteen minutes with them to say goodbye. Then you must leave. You must not go into the orphanage. These are our children.'

This was the stark message we received. For us, it was particularly painful. It meant leaving the children behind, putting them back into the situation where they had been. We felt that we had failed them. We felt we were letting them down. I really wanted to say to this attitude:

'No! These are not your children. Not the children we brought back. These are your children' – showing the photos of the children as they had been before they came to Ireland. But we had to remain diplomatic and calm.

We sat around to let the message sink in. The children must stay here and we must leave. Not even visiting rights. Through all this drama I have been the director, the official representative of Burren Chernobyl Project. The one who has to keep a cool head, to keep an eye on what is important, to stay unemotional in very emotional situations. The one to keep calm, to keep focused on the point in question, to maintain a certain dignity, to try to send love and positivity where there is none. Where there is hatred let us sow love. Let us sow love! When I have been upset and wanted to cry for Sergei, there were times when I could not. Now again, a time to keep a cool head. So, I will always, always be grateful to Theresa from Wexford for the round swears she let fly as we sat around in that office pondering on the situation. It certainly expressed what I was feeling at a particular level.

We went across the road to the orphanage to gather our bits and pieces. Load them in to the van and take them to the little house in Chapaeva Lane. We would have to squeeze in there for now. We went to the children to say goodbye. We didn't know for how long. How can this be happening? This is the bed we took Sergei out of three years ago and now we have brought him back three years later to place him back in it. It is the former Sergei I see in my arms as I lay him down in the bed. I smell the smells. I see the colours as it was then. And my heart breaks within me. I cannot do this! Three years! A Christ-journey to what? To another death? Another living death? Around me the workers, the Mamas, are in tears as news seeps through that we must leave, that we are not allowed in. I put Sergei back in his bed in group four and I know for a moment sheer and absolute panic. Despair as I see him as he was. And I whom he trusts am the one to put him back into the cot, into the hunger, into the life that he had. And I did it and I walked out.

Later I would kneel by my bed couch, squeeze his prayer-teddy and pray for him

Before I lay me down to sleep

I pray the Lord his soul to keep – and his body and his mind and his little heart –

The angels watch him in the night

Until he wakes in morning light. Amen.

We headed for our little house. Time for a coffee. For something to eat. Time to think. To think what to do. If we can't see the children there is not much point in staying here. Better go home and finish the adoption process for those in that situation. But no point just hanging around here.

The phone rang as we were digesting this latest twist to events. It was a doctor from the orphanage. He had news that a special commission of doctors was on the way to the orphanage to examine the children. He needed the photos of the children as they had been so that the doctors would appreciate the change. By the time we got back up to the orphanage, these doctors had finished their inspections and called us into their room. There was no question, they said, but that the children were in excellent shape. They were amazed at their condition. Everything was above board and without any possibility that the children had been in any way treated unwisely or unwell. They had this report prepared in writing and all four of them signed it. Thank God! But what a day! First we must leave the orphanage. Now, the doctors' report pleads with us to stay and continue the good work we have been doing. What to think!

We do not see the children next day, Saturday. Instead we take food to the entrance hut for them and the staff take it in and look after the children. This will be the pattern over the next several days. Now on this Saturday, we get news that another commission of doctors is on its way and that the children will be examined again. And again we are positive. We know this will be another positive report. And then they tell us that there will be another very special commission of people arriving on Monday for another examination. How many reports do they need?

Our women, having decided to return to Ireland, are making preparation for the journey. They will leave tomorrow so this is a sad day. For Caitriona it is a miserable, sad day. Theresa and Sheila are in Minsk with Br Lawrence. They could not stay around, so near and without access to the children. So, on Sunday we go to the airport to see off these gallant, heart-broken women. It is hard to grasp the emotion of the moment – not fear or loss, not anger or bitterness, just a sense of profound inability to believe that people here could not or would not understand that this was about children and about love. It was not about rules and regulations. Can they not see? Do they not understand? And apparently, they do not.

On Monday we waited for the extra special commission to arrive from Minsk. This was day three without seeing the children. In the morning, I took the food to the entrance-hut for the children. For all the staff it is a big shock and a disgrace the way things are working out. They have seen the improvements in the children. Why bring them back now? There is no way they will get the same treatment here. There are no such supports here as we have in Ireland. Why bring them back? For the children in all the units, fear that we won't be there for them anymore has spread like a cold wet fog through their fragile hearts and minds. They are afraid.

The commission of experts arrived at ten o'clock. They spent several hours with the children and in the orphanage grounds. I was in our little house. At ten to four, the phone rang. It was the deputy-director of the orphanage. He asked me to come to the office. I walked through the beautiful snowy park to the office. There were twelve to fifteen people sitting behind tables around the room. I expected an interrogation. A man approached as I entered. He introduced himself and his assistant. He is Governor of Minsk Region. They sat me between them and began to thank me sincerely and personally for all we had done for the children, for the orphanage. They hoped that we would continue to work there and that there would be better and further contact between us. They had seen with their own eyes what we had done and the exceptional results in the lives of the children.

Again another fine report. Head of Dermatology, Head of Paediatrics, Head of every discipline was here, all writing down the full positive results of their findings. An opportunity to speak, to contribute was offered to everyone. Only words of praise for our work in the orphanage were spoken by all. Words of thanks. Gratitude from those who knew how the place had been before we arrived.

So another period of waiting began. Loretto and Viv were still here with me. All the others were at home. Teresa had arrived back from Africa to an empty house, an idle beanbag lifeless on the floor. Sheila had gone back to an empty house, both Andrei's and Krystyna's rooms silent and soundless. Caitriona, gentle, quiet, professional soul, had gone home heart-broken, the leaving of Alosha a constant sob within her. Theresa Kehoe from Wexford had mustered her strength and, though vowing never to leave Vitalic, had changed her mind and headed home to make things happen quicker on the adoption side of things.

Here, we just kept going, visiting the children, bringing them food; reminding them who we were and who they were. Each day brought something new to wait for, to hope for. The staff, without question, were on our side and could not understand why the children were not allowed back with us to Ireland. A sob of dread, of loneliness, of fear was still shivering its way through the groups of children as they got wind of the word that there were still problems, that we were not allowed free access. They huddled in anxiety that we might go away and not come back. They seemed to understand our frustration. When we met Valeri on the street, he said: 'Liam, I miss you.' It was that simple, that simple what we meant to the children. So it was for all the units, all the children. They were aware of the cloud of uncertainty which had descended like a November mist and lay motionless over our naked hearts, awaiting the puff of care and love that would blow it all away.

Each morning I brought Sergei's bottles and feed for the other children to the orphanage gate. The workers on duty were embarrassed and confused that I was not allowed in. Yet they could not make the decision to open the gate. Instead, I handed in the packages to Maxim or to whichever of the staff was passing in to work and they would bring it to group four. On a few occasions, Lena the chemist in the orphanage came to the gate to meet me to ask for money for medication for some of the sick children. And so we waited in pure stupidity. In unbelief. In acceptance that this is Belarus. They do things their way. Each evening I collected the bottles from the gatehouse and headed back to our house to peel more carrots and potatoes for the following day's feeds. Having little to do was strange and made the day long, a day broken only by the routine of feed preparation. So, we waited.

Things returned somewhat to normal with the Director's arrival back. We could visit the children each day and spend time with them. Yet, one of the head nurses came to me very shyly one morning to say that a child had to go to hospital for blood analysis tests. She had asked for the orphanage car but they told her there was no money for petrol. She needed three thousand roubles, about a dollar and a half, to get the child to hospital. Without this dollar and a half, could a life have been lost? One wonders what a handicapped child's life is actually worth in Belarus? A dollar and a half.

So life again became a routine. With some spare time on hand, we began to think what else we needed to do on this trip. Our other projects also needed attention. Time to get busy with those. One of the things we had planned at the beginning of this trip was to revisit Sergei's mother in jail in Gomel. We had since learned that she had been moved to another prison not far from there but somewhere out in the countryside. We tried to make contact and bring Sergei to meet his mother again. So on Friday 29th, we got permission to go with Ina from the orphanage and Raisa as interpreter. Artur was our driver again. I had Sergei's bottles ready for the day and several changes of clothes, just in case of accidents on the way. It was a three and a half hour journey. We met Sergei's mother, Natasha. She is somewhat more serious. There is something about her that is different. She has hope in her eyes – hope that soon she will be free. Perhaps next summer. Perhaps sooner. The Governor of the jail is a wonderful man who insists that the women look like women, that they dress in their own clothes and not in prison garb and that they wear make-up. 'You are women, you must look like women!' He insists that his workers do work. Otherwise they are fired. A very serious deep-bassed boss of a man who is a great credit to himself and what he believes. Such a rarity here it seems to me.

We had a minor exhaust problem with the car on the return trip but were back in Cherven before too late. We had Sergei back in his bed in group four at about nine o'clock. The other children were settled for the night. One of the staff had little Paulina in her arms and was trying to give her a little fluid. Paulina was white, pure white. There would be no need for any more feeding, I thought. They called the medical staff as we were leaving after settling Sergei into his bed. A few moments later we phoned from the house to say that if there was anything at all Paulina needed and that could be got, to get it whatever it was, whatever it cost.

Next morning in the house, the phone rang. It was Natasha telling us the news. Paulina was dead. Paulina died just after eleven o'clock that night in her bed straight in from the door in group four, on the right, near the window. Thank God for her to be free from the prison of her broken body. She is at peace with the angels. But, need she have died? Was it just not being cared for? Not being fed suitable food? We had not done enough. We could scratch the name of four-year-old Paulina from our invitation list to Ireland. Another invitation had come for her. She would not be visiting with us.

I went up to the orphanage as usual with bottles of food for Sergei. I looked across at Paulina's empty bed. The green sheets from Ireland neat and tidy. It was feeding-time. The workers were busy. Three Mamas for thirty children – now twenty-nine children. I began to feed Sergei his bottles of Ready Brek with honey and olive oil. I looked again towards Paulina's empty bed, to think of her, to wish her well, to say a prayer, to say sorry we had not done more. Had anyone even held her in her last moments?

In group four, the beds are in rows of two. Two beds side by side. Side by side by Paulina's bed a Mama was sitting on the edge feeding the boy who slept there. Two beds together, one Paulina's, one his. Just then, one of the big boys, Maxim, came in with one of the medical staff. He walked over to what I had thought was an empty bed. He gracefully lifted the little bundle of Paulina's remains wrapped in Subbutteo table green cloth into his arms and took her out. A freeze-frame moment! A Mama is sitting on the edge of a bed feeding a small boy side by side with the dead body of a little girl. Porridge. *Casha.* Soup.

It cannot be! It cannot be! Paulina's little remains cannot have been there. All the time. In the bed. Beside him. Eating breakfast. Maxim. Bundle in his arms. Going out. Sergei sucking his bottle. Green. It cannot be. Yet, it is!

* * *

We had no sense of what was happening in the outside world, the real world. This had become our reality. Minding children. Minding ourselves. Paying bills. Waiting. Trying to see sense in all of it. Why were we here? The return of the children over one month ago had not been to their advantage. No-one really wanted them back for themselves. But here we are, five weeks in and nothing has improved. There is no progress for them. And the other children we want to bring out are in a limbo-world of green-wrapped uncertainty. There are attitudes here hard to understand. While we love Belarus and its so-friendly people with their amazing hospitality, and while we have been welcomed with open arms by so many, yet there is still something difficult to understand. There is a different attitude. A different approach to some things. Especially in relation to the handicapped. It is hard to reconcile with the beauty and welcome of the people. Yet it is there. But we can only observe and offer our help. We certainly cannot throw stones from our past at anyone. Simply try to understand and try to help.

Raisa had been with us to help interpret in the hope that we could make some progress. She was also helping to arrange visits to Ireland for children from Yastrebel Orphanage for normal children as well as a visit of some children from families. One of the ones we wanted to bring this year was poor Jenka's sister whom we had met at his funeral. Raisa phoned his mother to explain what documents she needed to prepare. She tried to explain this over the phone. She called out the instructions and Jenka's mother wrote down what she needed to do. The line was bad and sometimes Raisa had to shout out the instructions, sometimes even having to spell out the words. Half-way through she looked at us and said, 'She cannot write it, the electricity had gone.' So we chatted a little. Then Raisa said, 'It's Ok, they've got a candle.'

After that Raisa headed off on the bus to go back to Goradishche to continue feeding the children there. It was a Monday.

We followed on the next morning. It was Tuesday 3 December, the day of Invalids in Belarus. On this day, the *internats* or orphanages are open to the public. Visitors may come to see the children. The hope is that they come with toys and presents. We loaded the car with sweets for all the children and with toys for everyone, enough for the children in the Minsk Day Centre and plenty for Goradishche as well. Viv would look after Cherven and see that all the children there got something each on this day. I headed off with Artur to do the other two places. In Minsk the centre is going well and the interest taken by the parents of the children is what is making a real difference. The children there are thriving and learning. It is a place of progress, a place of hope. We left toys and sweets for everyone there and set off for Goradishche orphanage, near Baranovichi, two hours away.

The snow had come, the first real signs of the Russian winter, a winter which can plummet to minus thirty-five or more. Thirty-five degrees of frost, as they say. Yet it is a dry cold, different to what we get on the Atlantic coast. And they cope with these winters. On our trip, all the roads were open. The last hill down Goradishche was a little bit dicey but no problems otherwise. Raisa would be at the orphanage feeding the children in all the units there. The children got bananas and yogurts. After arrival, we got word that she was somewhere in one of the units out the back. So we set off to find her. When we found her, we met up with another shock.

'Liam, I can't do this anymore. It's better to go back to school.'

'What?'

'You know Liam, Nastia has died. Nastia who was in Ireland with Jim and Teresa Willis in Ennis. She died on Saturday. They buried her on Sunday. No-one came. None of her parents or family. They came only looking for the burial money. And she was fine. When I was here on Wednesday and Thursday, she ate all her banana, all her yogurt. She ate everything. It's awful!'

Raisa is a powerful woman, a mighty woman as we would say in Clare. It is the first time I have seen her so upset. She had come to Cherven to help out with interpreting. Now she is upset that she was not here when Nastia died. Beautiful Nastia. With her little smile. A beautiful child whom Jim and Teresa loved in Ennis when she was there. Oh! How will I tell them? It is over a year now that we have been asking for her return to Ireland and the authorities in Brest will not give permission. Another heartbreak. Another beautiful child gone unloved into the grave. We do not expect to keep them all alive but there was genuine five-star love in the Willis house for Nastia. She was one of the family. How will I tell them? I cannot! Each death a body-blow. Each death a failure. Where in the name of Jesus are you, Jesus? Where? Where? Where? Why? Why are we here? Why did she die? We have been trying and trying and trying so hard! She was so beautiful when she came back. And she had come to know Jim and Teresa and their gorgeous children. Oh! Why?

Later, we were told that they didn't even have the price of a coffin for her. So they made a box. But I was in Cherven! You knew that! I had stupid money! Died on a Saturday! Buried on the Sunday! In a bloody box! Oh! Sweet Jesus!

In group three, in the second small room to the right where Nastia had had her bed, her toys were still in place. On her bed was the musical toy which you wind up and it plays a beautiful little lullaby tune. I wound it up over her empty bed and thought of Jim and Teresa and the children in Ennis. On the wall is Winnie-the-Pooh and Eeyore stickers which Jim had stuck up on his last visit. 'She's gorgeous, isn't she?' I remember Jim saying. Gorgeous.

The heating broke down when the frosts came, they say. They say she got an infection on Friday. She had the doctor on Saturday several times. She died. How many more must die this year? First Jenka in Ireland. Then Vera's daughter in Cherven town. Then Artum in Goradishche. Then the teenager in Goradishche. Then the call back of the children. Then Paulina in

Cherven. Then Nastia in Goradichche. What is set loose among us? Will it never end? Where there is hatred, let us sow love. Let us sow love. Let us love. Love.

It was then that it seemed to me that Sergei wanted me to write just what I felt he would have wished to say. This is what I felt was coming from his spirit:

Just a short note from Cherven Orphanage in Belarus. A note to thank you for listening to my story when I came to Clare three years ago. The photograph you saw of me then is no longer me. But it was me. And there were so many more like me, whom no-one could love. It is difficult out here. But you looked at that photograph and heard our story and then did something about it. Some of you gave money and some sent clothes and some said prayers and some sent love. Some took us into their hearts and some came to visit us. And where there was indifference, you sowed love. And where there was poverty, you sowed love. And where there was nothing, you sowed love. And in the room where I had lain for several months with twenty-six others, you sowed life. And I am alive because of you. And Vika is alive. And Alosha is alive and well and at home. And Dasha went to Ireland and Veronica went to Ireland and Sasha went to Ireland. And Jenka had three beautiful years in Killaloe and he went to heaven. And more of you came. And new clothes came. And clean beds came. And joy of joys, food and nappies came.

And, when you first came to our unit, people wondered how you could look at us. And they wondered how you could want us. And they are still puzzled why you love us. Why do you love us? In our various ways, we all know that you love us. And, since we came back, every Ministry here is aware that we exist and that people want us to go abroad. There was no system to allow us to go abroad before but, now, there soon will be, thanks to you. And more of us will travel to Ireland and some of us will go to Clare. And when we do arrive there, maybe there will be someone there to love us again – a Martina or a Jim or maybe a Teresa whom I miss so much.

Don't be sad for us.

Be strong for us.

Sow love somewhere today.
Sow life.
Sow more life.

Sergei
Cherven Orphanage, Belarus
and formerly of Miltown Malbay, Co Clare.

* * *

Now we wait for the new legislation. We wait with pining hearts for the return of the children. We wait in the hope that many others in serious need will also be allowed to travel to Ireland, to the many groups around the country who care for them. We know that, in the long term, the solution will have to be found in Belarus. We draw on the strength within us to continue the work, to continue to be open to the spirit which drives us and which draws us. We continue to love Belarus, its beautiful people and its beautiful children. Our hope is that we can give back to them a little of the love and the joy they have brought to our lives, because they have touched us in a special way, in tender places.

They have brought us to an understanding of what love is. We want to go back to them and to be with them. We want to be with the children and the people of Belarus. Together, let us continue to sow love.

But also as we wait, we ponder. In the midst of the trauma and heart-tugs, there is time to think. Where is the call of the Lord in all of this? What is it that the Spirit of the Universe asks of us now? The children came to us and we were delighted. Now the children have called us back into their world. The mountain to Mohammed, Mohammed to the mountain. The workers and staff of the orphanage have been wonderful in their welcome and in trying to create miracles in their poverty. New systems are now in place. The pain-grit in our hearts must now become oystered pearl as we slowly come to hear the call for us to once again come and see. The call is to focus not just on the seven who have been with us but the seven times seventy children. Let us lead on in more love and more hope. And in great thanks for it all.

CHAPTER EIGHTEEN

They had not understood about the loaves

The figure of a little child being held in the palm of a hand is our symbol of who we are. Made by Susan Minogue of Tulla, these are very beautiful figures and capture for us the essence of what we are about. Wherever we go, we leave one of these. To people who help us, we give a little figure of a child being held tenderly and lovingly in the palm of a hand. This is a powerful image, an image given to us in our Bible: 'I have carved you on the palm of my hand.' It carries a Divine promise for all of us, a promise that we will never be forgotten. This powerful symbol has sustained and carried generation after generation, soul after soul, making us able to continue, to persevere, not to give up. We have the promise that no matter what the circumstances, we are images of God, carved on his hand. We are not just held, we are carved on the palm of God. These beautiful lines go on to remind us that just as a mother never forgets her baby, as a woman never forgets the child within her womb, even more so with God. Even if such strange wonders came about that a woman might forget her child or a mother forget the baby within her womb, even so God will not forget us. The Spirit is with us, available to us, loving us.

I can only write about the children I have come to know and speak on behalf of the ones who have no voice. There are of course many children in Belarus taken from their parents because these parents were unable or unfit to look after children – due to alcohol, poverty or violence. There are some parents who have had to make the difficult choice of letting their child go to an *internat* because there are no home helps, no real state supports. The mother is often left on her own and she must work in order to survive. There is no way she can afford to pay someone while she works and no way both can survive on the small state pension given for a handicapped child. It is true that by our standards nowadays many of these children in the orphanages could lead a normal life and should not be in an institution at all. All they need is a little support. Yet, it is the reality of where they live and where they will live out their lives. There is no real way out of the system at this time.

A few years ago, I knew very little about handicapped children, how they lived, how they were educated, what they needed. Now I understand the living fear of the parents of handicapped children who have no security about the safe future of their child when they, the parents, pass on. Where will the child live? Who will look after him/her? When discussing this with Olga and Tamara in Minsk, I suggested that maybe it is better if their child dies before the parents. They said together: 'Liam, it is better if it is on the same day.'

Right now, we in Ireland are facing our own past. We are opening the back rooms, searching the attics and dark places and letting the light into our own past, into the *internats*, orphanages and children's homes. For me, it is like being in a time warp. On one side I am visiting children who are unwanted and rejected. I am welcomed by each and all of them, in the hope that with me comes sweets, help, presents, warmth and love. On the other side, I am one of a group of Christian Brothers who are blamed, to put it mildly, for the unforgivable in institutions in Ireland. Let it be understood that unforgivable things did happen in the past. Unforgivable things are still happening to children in so many places. It is a strange position. Welcomed in Belarus, blamed in Ireland, being friends with Paddy who was raised in an institution until adopted. Strange times. Strange situation. But we must face the truth. We must change the truth which is our truth if that truth has been camouflaged in alleged care where there was no care; in controlling ritual where ritual took control; in hypocritical persons for whom a child didn't really matter. We must face it and change it.

So, I try to listen to the cry of the past, to somehow understand and be aware of the hurts. I also know the wonderful, generous, beautiful men who have been Christian Brothers down the years. Men who have given of their soul's blood to enable others to have a life and make something of their lives. Yes, there were the warped ones as there are in any family but to

have lived with some of the great ones, great of giving and belief! Men whose inspiration came from a crucified servant on a
cross, men who followed their star and kept their light of
humanity glowing, men whose souls now ache with the very
thought that children under our collective care were abused.
Now a shock-stone has been dropped raw into our hearts and
we feel the sear of failure to those in our care, of failure to ourselves, of failure to the Lord. And some cannot think for the
cockcrow that resounds in our hearts. There are so many loyal
believers who also feel this hurt. Something they had believed in
has been shown to have been so much talk and so untrue behind
the scenes. It feels again like Tatiana saying of the Communist
system: 'It was all a lie.' And the tragedy is that it wasn't. Not all
of it. Yet, we know that no going back will relieve the hurt ones,
nothing can really make up for trust and hope and love treasoned
and all we have left is our sorrow. And my sorrow goes to those
hurt and to the good people whose spirit was right, who gave of
themselves again selflessly in another time and another world,
in a time when the last thing professed was humanity and love.
And I feel the ripple of hurt from these great men, generous
souls, light of the world. Men of love.

And yet can we men ever understand what it is to be a frightened child? What am I not seeing now when I walk into an orphanage? Can we celibate men ever understand what it is to have
a son or daughter and have that child abused by a trusted person? Or by a person known not to be trustworthy where children
are concerned? A pity it will be if our sorrow at the revelations
from the past now gets in the way of seeing and feeling the hurt
of the little sparrows under our care. Theirs is a much greater
hurt and a much greater crucifixion than anything we can feel. It
must not be the revelations that hurt us now but the things that
went on unseen or tolerated. And it must be faced and recognised and healed. Because in other times and other places it is
still going on. And I can name today children dying of starvation.
It is not enough to say sorry for the past. We must seek and hopefully receive forgiveness. Saying sorry is a mere beginning.
Restitution and forgiveness must follow. Only then is there a
small hope of healing. It must happen. Because there are now
children with different names in the same situation and worse.

Problems are still with us. For someone visiting orphanages at this stage they will usually find that bits of paper are more important than children. 'You cannot give him vitamins unless a doctor signs a paper. We cannot burn these old clothes as someone will check the list and we will have to answer for it. We cannot move this child to hospital as you need to get a form filled. She is starving but she cannot get more food as these are the norms. He cannot be changed now as he is changed three times a day. He will die. She will die. He doesn't want to eat. It is his disease. It is her disease. Can she be moved to hospital? Yes, but who will look after her? Can she get milk? Yes if the doctor says so. There is no milk. There is nothing for them to do – but they are able to do nothing. Why are they in a small bed? Because their legs are twisted. Why are their legs twisted? Because they are in a small bed.'

We each need love. We need to know that we are beautiful in someone's eyes and to see that beauty reflected in the eyes of those who love us. In the eyes of many handicapped children we are beautiful. They ask for little, they wait to see. We try to interpret their needs and to bring love, wonder and activity where there was disdain, boredom and listlessness. It bothered me that there were so many children there whom I believe could read and write but who never got the chance to learn. It bothered me that their basic right to an education was not being granted. It was Tony who said to me that teaching these children to read and write might not be the most important thing in the world. The handicapped ones have far more to teach us than we have to teach them. They are far more important in the world than in just being there to be taught. Their lessons for us are much bigger than that.

Life is changing. It has changed. Religious life is changing. Isn't it about time! We need to think and to re-view. We need to throw out the nonsense, the bandages of ritual and legalism which enwrapped the healthy spirit and made it lifeless and sterile. It may be time to throw everything out and begin again. We must be free. When I worked in Luninets in southern Belarus, I went for a walk every evening. Several months into my time there, I was introduced to a local man. He said he knew who I was. When I wondered how, he said he had seen me walk-

FALLOUT

ing. He knew I was a foreigner. 'But how did you know?' I asked. His reply was, 'Everything about you said freedom.' As people of a loving God, everything about us must say freedom.

Nowadays, we try to be free. We are told we must learn to 'be'. We are not human doings, we are human beings. Nice and clever but just 'being' is not enough. There are many, many, hungry, starving children in our world. You still want to just 'be'? 'The faith of Abraham was active along with his deeds and became perfect by what he did.' (Jas 3:22) Luckily, nowadays, it is possible to be a missionary at home and from home. The world has opened up and become smaller in some ways. This also means there is no excuse any more for not doing something. There is no excuse for a starving child or a starving country anywhere in our present world. No excuse. We cannot say we are unaware. We all know. Time to do something. Time to declare war on hunger and poverty. It is time.

To do something means taking responsibility for ourselves and our actions. We cannot just accept inherited wisdom and practice without making them our own. This is the real responsibility. Tradition can be good or bad. We need to mould it to our times, to accept responsibility for our own actions. We cannot say any more, 'The serpent tempted me and I ate.' In other words, I was guided by someone else. We cannot just accept what is given to us and eat. We must decide for ourselves. Ned Crosby puts it very well when he writes: 'For the first time in my life, I realise that, apart from a few years of childhood, I had always accepted handouts for the maintenance of my soul.'

It is time to take responsibility for the maintenance of our souls. For the maintenance of the physical and spiritual well-being of this planet. It is time to harness the eternal echoes resounding within us. It is time to be the person we want to be, to do the things we need to do, to be who we are. It is time.

In the eyes of God we are all special needs. When we return to him, we will be welcome if we come not in power or majesty, we need not even come intact. We will be welcome and have done well if we return home from the fallout of life's journey with our love in fragments.